THE METAPHYSICS OF EXPERIENCE

THE METAPHYSICS OF EXPERIENCE

LESLIE STEVENSON

CLARENDON PRESS · OXFORD

1982

Oxford University Press, Walton Street, Oxford OX2 6DP
London Glasgow New York Toronto
Delhi Bombay Calcutta Madras Karachi
Kuala Lumpur Singapore Hong Kong Tokyo
Nairobi Dar es Salaam Cape Town
Melbourne Auckland
and associates in
Beirut Berlin Ibadan Mexico City Nicosia

Published in the United States by
Oxford University Press, New York

British Library Cataloguing in Publication Data
Stevenson, Leslie
The Metaphysics of Experience
1. Experience
1. Title
121   BD181
ISBN 0-19-824655-2
ISBN 0-19-824699-4 paperback

Library of Congress Cataloging in Publication Data
Stevenson, Leslie Forster.
The metaphysics of experience.
Includes bibliographical references.
1. Knowledge, Theory of. 2. Experience.
3. Perception (Philosophy) 4. Judgment.
5. Causation. I. Title.
BD161.S683   121   82-3525
ISBN 0-19-824655-2   AACR2
ISBN 0-19-824699-4 paperback

Typeset on a Rank Xerox 850 Word Processor by Susan Jones
Printed in Great Britain by
Thomson Litho Ltd, East Kilbride, Scotland
bound by
Oxford University Press

To ZINAIDA

PREFACE

I come not to exhume Kant, but to resurrect him. This work is inspired by the Critique of Pure Reason, yet is not about it: perhaps over-ambitiously, I try to delineate not Kant's metaphysics of experience but the truth of the matter. It seemed to me tedious to turn out yet another work of Kant scholarship, and a better bicentenary tribute to his genius to engage in reconstruction rather than archaeology on the monument he left us (fortunately, with works of the mind, doing one does not exclude doing the other). At the end of the Preface to the second edition, Kant said that although aware of the obscurities in his Critique, he must, because of his advancing years, leave the elaboration and elucidation of his system to "those worthy men who have made my teaching their own". Given the very radical nature of the reconstructions I propose, I can hardly hope to receive such (posthumous) blessing from the master. But I like to think that he would approve the effort to pursue the subject further in a systematic way, and would prefer that our motto be not just 'Back to Kant!' but 'Forward from Kant!'

In my pursuit of the necessary conditions for any conceivable experience I have used many ideas from the mainstream of contemporary analytical philosophy. I have found the work of Wittgenstein crucial, and it may well be said that there is as much of him as there is of Kant in my results. But I am not attempting to add to the already highly developed Wittgenstein industry, which threatens to churn out a heap of scholarship to rival that under which Kant lies buried. Other giants on whose shoulders I have stood are acknowledged in the notes. The books most akin to mine in over-all project are, P.F. Strawson's The Bounds of Sense (1966), Wilfrid Sellars' Science and Metaphysics: Variations On Kantian Themes (1968), Ross Harrison's On What There Must Be (1974), and Jay F. Rosenberg's One World and Our Knowledge of It (1980), the last of which came to my notice too late for my proper digestion but which I warmly recommend as a further treatment of this subject. I do not however, require my readers to be familiar with all this recent philosophical output, or indeed with Kant's own text. I have tried hard to present the ideas and arguments, wherever they come from, in as clear and forthright a style as possible, undisguised with scholarly camouflage. All names, references, and comments on other people's work are banished to the notes at the end of the book, and might be reserved for a second reading (if there is one). In particular, I show rather than say where I agree and disagree with the first Critique, in so far as I understand that profound but obscure, over-systematic yet carelessly written, inspiring and infuriating, magnificent but flawed masterpiece. Cognoscenti of Kant and his recent commentators in English will, with the aid of the notes, be able to discover my tracks. (Some shorter studies of mine, from which the present work evolved, are published elsewhere.)*

I have attempted a highly systematic presentation, in which the very form of the work reflects the content of the arguments. Kant is often derided for the extent to which he allows his penchant for architectonic structure to distort his insights, but I think that he had the right instinct in assuming that there must be some systematic way in which the necessary conditions for experience fit together. The

Preface

contemporary trend in analytical philosophy seems to be towards ever more specialized, jargon-infested (and, dare we say it, unreadable) work, and there is, I think, a need to draw things together into a wider view which can be more generally appreciated. In attempting the painting of such a large picture in a small space, and in allowing the canvas to go on public view in its present state, I am keenly aware that many of the details remain sketchy and will be found disputable. I hope others will be not merely provoked to punch holes, but inspired to repair them with better material.

I am grateful to the University of St. Andrews for the opportunities for teaching and research it has given me (particularly for six months' study leave in 1980), and to my colleagues in the Department of Logic and Metaphysics (especially Crispin Wright) for their critical scrutiny of my half-formed ideas.

St. Andrews
August 1981

* "Recent Work on the Critique of Pure Reason", The Philosophical Quarterly 29 (1979); "Three Kinds of Transcendental Idealism", in Akten des 5. Internationales Kant-Kongresses, ed. G. Funke, Mainz, 1981; "Things in Themselves and Scientific Explanation", Indian Philosophical Quarterly 8 (1981); "Wittgenstein's Transcendental Deduction and Kant's Private Language Argument", Kant-Studien (forthcoming).

CONTENTS

Contents

Contents

Chapter One

NECESSARY CONDITIONS FOR EXPERIENCE

In this study, we inquire into what is necessary for experience.[1] Our investigation is directed not towards phenomena, but to the possibilities of experiencing phenomena.[2] It is not any kind of empirical examination of the nature of things, nor is it merely analysis of the meanings of terms; it is rather, an elucidation of what is required for there to be experience of anything at all.

1.1 **EXPERIENCE**

We must do our best to explain the notion of experience used in these opening definitions. The word has a common use in English to mean knowledge, skill, or wisdom acquired from life and practice over a substantial period of time. Such temporal and mnemic connotations will take on increasing importance as our argument proceeds, but our initial use of the term 'experience' is that which has featured so centrally in modern epistemology, namely to refer to the momentary states of consciousness of an individual perceiver and thinker. In this philosophical usage, which is also in common speech, the term has a plural, as in 'I've had several peculiar experiences today.'

All that we assume about experience is that it involves both perception and thought. That is any subject of experience has, on our definition, both sensibility (the capacity for sensory awareness) and understanding (the ability to make judgments about what he is aware of).[3]

1

1.11 **Intuitions**

All experience is thus <u>of</u> something, in the sense that the experiencer can, as a thinker, put some description or classification on the content of his experience. But we do not <u>assume</u> that every, or even any, experience must be of an object or state of affairs distinct from the present state of the subject. (Such questions will be discussed in 4.) So the "sensibility" which is one half of our definition of experience covers not only the perception that a visible cat is miaowing, or that the weather is cold, but also the hallucination of a dagger before one, and the awareness of a toothache, or of an uneasy feeling that something dreadful is going to happen.

The term 'intuition' can be used with the same reference as 'experience', but with a sense which picks out the <u>sensory</u> aspect in the very general way just suggested; it will thus mean any awareness of a particular present item or state, whether external or internal. It may be questioned how appropriate it is to lump together perception (and mis-perception) of external things with hallucinations, and with awareness of one's own sensations, emotions, and thoughts. We shall be making distinctions later (in 5 and 6); all we are assuming now is that, whether or however such distinctions are drawn, the notion of experience includes "intuition" - the awareness of (at least subjective) particulars.

1.12 **Concepts**

The other half of our definition of experience is "understanding" - the ability to make judgments about the contents of experience. Judgments are paradigmatically expressed by assertions, which are speech-acts in some language, but our use of the term 'judgment' covers mental acts of recognizing, noticing, and realizing, whether or not they are overtly expressed. But just as any assertion must employ at least one general term, so any judgment must apply at least one concept - where a "concept" is something essentially general or universal, applicable to more than one case.

In saying or thinking that a particular item or state is thus-and-so, we are classifying it, assigning it to a certain kind, implying that it is similar in the relevant respect to other actual or possible cases. We must therefore be following a rule, in the minimal sense that it makes sense to raise the question whether this particular act of judging is correct. Any assertion or judgment has some definite content, that things are so-and-so rather than such-and-such; it is therefore assessable as right or wrong.

1.13 Sensibility and Understanding

Neither sensibility nor understanding may be eliminated without loss of our intended subject-matter. It may well be claimed that a fish can perceive a fly, and see that it is moving downstream, without <u>thinking</u> of the fly or <u>judging</u> that anything is the case. We do not deny that in one sense of 'experience' many creatures incapable of assertion, judgment, or thought can have, enjoy, or suffer various kinds of experience (including sensations and perceptions). We just point out that our subject-matter here is the experience of rational beings, who can apply concepts to their intuitions and thus make judgments about what they are aware of. Exactly what is implied in these notions of "rationality", "concept", and "judgment" will be examined in more detail later (in 3).

On the other hand, it may be suggested that a divine (or at least disembodied) intelligence could entertain thoughts and make judgments, even perhaps about particular perceptible things, but without material sense-organs and therefore with no capacity literally to <u>perceive</u> anything. Those unsympathetic to such theological or metaphysical speculation may yet be inclined to ascribe such understanding without sensibility to actual or possible computers. It is pertinent in either case to press the question of what would give meaning to the attribution of the relevant concepts to the supposed rational being, in the absence of any possibility of it applying its concepts to a particular case because it stands in a relevant perceptual relation to the instance. How, for example, can we say that a chess-playing computer thinks its queen is threatened, unless we can also attribute to it perception of the state of play, on the ground that it reacts appropriately (by moving or defending its queen) when it is fed with information about the situation on the board implying that its opponent could take its queen next move? Even if we do not presuppose the existence of an external world, and try to conceive of a rational being making judgments about nothing else but its own internal states, we have still to assume that it makes a present-tense singular judgment <u>because</u> it is in some sense aware of a <u>particular</u> present state which is the topic of that judgment. It thus has "intuitions" in the very general sense intended here.

"Intuitions without concepts are blind, concepts without

intuitions are empty. The understanding can intuit nothing, the senses can think nothing. Only through their union can knowledge arise."[4]

1.2 NECESSARY CONDITIONS

The conditions we are concerned with are those logically or conceptually necessary for experience. If it is physically necessary for such experience that there be so many million neurones (or equivalent functional units) with certain complicated patterns of interconnection, supplied with blood (or other energy input), that is no business of ours. The subject-matter here is not the physics but the metaphysics of experience.

1.21 Transcendental Arguments

We thus aim to produce arguments of the form:

> There is experience;
> If there is experience, then ϕ;
> <u>ergo</u> ϕ;

where statements of the form of the second premiss are to express conceptual, not causal, connections. Clearly, the <u>modus</u> <u>ponens</u> form guarantees that any such argument is deductively valid.

It is possible to use the conclusion of any such argument as the premiss for further argument, of the form:

> ϕ
> If ϕ then ψ;
> <u>ergo</u> ψ;

where once again the second premiss is to express a conceptual connection, and the form is deductively valid.

Two arguments of the above forms can be compressed into a single argument of the first form (with ψ for ϕ). Any such argument starting from the premiss that there is experience (and hence any chain of arguments which can be compressed into this form) may be called a "transcendental argument".[5]

1.22 A Priori Knowledge

The premiss that there is experience has a peculiar epistemological status. If we are going in for any form of intelligible inquiry at all, we surely know that we are doing so, and are therefore entitled to assume at the outset that we have experience in the sense explained, involving sensibility and understanding.[6] If we know anything, we surely know this; and we know it in advance of knowing the specific contents of our experience. Our knowledge that there is experience is thus a priori,[7] and does not depend for its justification on what our experience turns out to be.

Yet whoever "we" are, it is surely a contingent fact that we exist at all, or have experience. Even if it is a defining feature of the species homo sapiens that normal members of it have the powers of perception and judgment, it is not a logical truth that creatures of our human species have evolved and still survive. If 'we' is understood to mean persons or rational beings, not necessarily humans, the existence of any such beings still seems to be a contingent matter. Whatever the reference of 'we', then, that we have experience is a contingent truth which we nevertheless know a priori, if we know – or think – anything at all.

It is even possible to go back to an individual rather than collective starting-point, namely the premiss 'I have experience' - expressing the thinker's knowledge (even if he doubts the existence of anything distinct from himself) that he can make judgments about items of which he is aware. The singular premiss has at least the same status as the one in the first-person plural, and many have thought it to be more certain.[8] In 4 we will therefore start from this position in which solipsism seems to be a possibility.

An apparently yet more minimal starting-point is suggested by our wording the first premiss of transcendental arguments as 'There is experience', rather than 'I have experience'. It has sometimes been claimed that the latter expresses a knowledge or awareness of <u>oneself</u> as the subject or owner of the present experience which is not implied by the mere knowledge that there <u>is</u> experience. Whether this is a genuine possibility must also be discussed later (in 4.2); our formulation here does not rule it out.

1.23 Conceptual Connections

Clearly, the real work in any transcendental argument is done by the second premiss, of the form 'If there is experience, then ϕ'. As already said, the conditions which we seek are those logically, rather than causally, necessary for experience. 'If ... then' connections of the relevant kind are thus established not by observation, experiment, or scientific theorizing, but by logical deduction from, or conceptual analysis of, what is meant by 'experience'. Our task is to deduce what we can from our assumption that experience involves both the awareness of particular items and the application of general concepts to them.

It is fairly obvious that any interesting inferences to be made here will not proceed merely by manipulations of logical forms which could be represented in a calculus; we will surely have to attempt some kind of analysis of the very notions of awareness, perception, judgment, and concept. That such analysis is far from trivial or obvious is suggested by the long history of philosophical discussion. We will not inquire further at this stage into the nature of the relevant conceptual connections - whether, for example, there is any important distinction to be drawn between entailment and pre-supposition. It is over-methodical to expect methodology always to precede method.[9]

1.24 The Synthetic A Priori

We have noted that the first premiss of transcendental arguments - the existence of experience - has the peculiar status of being knowable a priori while being only contingently true. And we have said that any relevant instances of the second premiss must express conceptual connections, and will therefore be necessarily true and, presumably, also knowable a priori (although as an empirical matter of human development, it may need very considerable experience and education before one can understand the sort of abstract reasoning involved in defending such propositions - but that, of course, is true of many necessary propositions, for example, those of higher mathematics). It is tempting to infer that the conclusions of transcendental arguments must inherit from their first premiss the status we have noted, which reminds us strongly of the traditional "synthetic a priori".

It would, however, be dangerous to assume that anything other than truth is guaranteed to be transmitted from premises to conclusion in a valid deductive argument. Yet since both premises of a transcendental argument are knowable a priori, and the argument is of the extremely simple and familiar modus ponens form, it seems reasonable to claim that the conclusion is also knowable a priori. But to claim that it is synthetic would commit us to taking a view about the defensibility and nature of the now controversial analytic-synthetic distinction, which we can hardly at this initial stage be entitled to do.

Fortunately, the interest of our inquiry does not depend on whether the controversial expression 'synthetic a priori' is exactly the right label to put on its results. We are not assuming that synthetic a priori propositions abound, and then asking how they are possible;[10] our premiss is merely that there is experience, and our question is how that is possible.[11] Our conclusions will, as argued, be knowable a priori; they will be true in any conceivable experience, and in any possible conceptual scheme, for they are independent of whatever perceptions or concepts that any particular rational being may have. So our results will be not just what we cannot (because of our actual human nature) help believing;[12] not merely the postulates, categories, or absolute presuppositions of a certain culture in one period of history;[13] not the present banks of "the river-bed of thought";[14] not even a "massive central core of human thinking" which has not as a matter of fact changed;[15] but the logically indispensable core of any conceptualized experience of any rational being, in any culture, place, and time. Our conclusions should therefore be accepted by the philosopher who tries to start by assuming nothing more than his own experience, by the linguist, historian, and anthropologist who essay to interpret a radically different culture (or even a species of extra-terrestrial rational beings), and by all of us in understanding each other.

Chapter Two

THE TEMPORALITY OF EXPERIENCE

We can try to start our inquiry by concentrating first on the premiss that experience involves sensibility, namely the capacity for awareness of particular items. We will find that time plays a more fundamental role than space.

2.1 TIME AS THE FORM OF SENSIBILITY

Does anything follow from the mere awareness of particular items or states? Remember that this abstract formulation is meant to cover not only the perception of material objects (dogs and trees, houses and hills) and objective states of affairs (that it is hot, raining, noisy, or smelly) but also the awareness of one's own mental states (sensations, desires, emotions, and thoughts). Material objects and states of the environment are of course located at publicly specifiable places and times (allowing for some vagueness about just where it ceases to be noisy or smelly), but mental states notoriously lack spatial positions or relations. No doubt the owner of the mental states must, as an embodied creature, always be somewhere, but we are at a stage of our inquiry at which solipsism has not yet been excluded, and so embodiment is not assumed. But it seems that even if the subject is doubtful of all "outer" or spatial relations, he can be aware of temporal relations between his experiences, for example, that a certain thought occurred <u>during</u> the persistence of that pain, and was <u>followed</u> by the yearning which he still feels <u>now</u>. It is not necessary, of course, that a subject consciously thinks

11

about the temporal relations between all his experiences; it is just that for any pair of them it makes sense for him to raise the question of their time-order, and the suggestion is that any pair of them must be either successive, overlapping, or simultaneous. This ordering is, for all we yet know, entirely private to the subject: it is the sequence of his experiences, not his experience of sequences.

If this conclusion is accepted, time may be said to be the necessary form of inner (as well as outer) sense. Philosophers have often been content to assume of inner (as well as outer) sense.[16] Philosophers have often been content to assume the temporality of experience as an unquestionable premiss,[17] even if they have been puzzled by the kind of necessity this truth seems to possess, and have sometimes been unable to persuade themselves that it is actually analytic that the very concept of experience involves that of time.[18] The logical possibility of non-temporal experience has however been suggested,[19] so the conception, however outré, must be considered.

Before we do so, let us note another argument for the necessary temporality of experience (related to that sketched above) which proceeds from the possible plurality of items of awareness to the need for some means for individuating items exactly similar in kind.[20] If we are not at this stage to make any assumptions about an outer world of material objects, it seems that we cannot presuppose spatial position as the ground of individuation for numerically different but qualitatively identical items, and must therefore use temporal relationships for this purpose. But perhaps this move is made too quickly, for does not the "spatial" arrangement of items within an unchanging visual field give us an example, even without assuming any public world, of the individuation of particulars by spatial rather than temporal positions? Could there not be awareness of a multiplicity of coloured shapes which were completely static, yet classifiable as of various general types? (Think, for example, of the visual experience one may have when one closes one's eyes in bright sunlight, and imagine it to be unchanging, and perhaps a good deal more complex.)[21] Does this not show the logical possibility of experience in which there is no change in the objects of awareness, and for which the premiss of our previous argument - that it must make sense to ask about the time-order of any two experiences - does not perhaps hold?

2.2 TIME AS THE FORM OF UNDERSTANDING

At this point we must realize that we cannot hope to deduce much about experience without considering its conceptual as well as its sensory aspect.[22] The notion of awareness which we have been using, although supposedly abstract enough to have both material things and one's own mental states as its objects, does at any rate imply some sort of conceptualization, some classification of particular items as of certain general kinds. Our talk of two or more things being recognizably similar although numerically distinct assumes this. So the question we are posing is: could there be experience involving judgments about the contents of awareness, but in which there is no succession or change whatsoever?

To answer this, we have to try to abstract from the fact that judgments, as we normally understand them, are mental acts which occur at fairly specific times;[23] we must ask whether in non-temporal experience there could be anything that deserves the names 'judgment', 'recognition', or 'classification'. One thing that is essential, if such notions are to apply, is the possibility of truth or falsity, correctness or incorrectness.[24] A judgment makes a claim, and unless there is the logical possibility of mistake or incorrectness, how can there be any claim at all? It might seem straight away that the notion of mistake cannot apply unless there is some possibility of detection, whether this takes the public form of correction by another language-user, or the private form of the subject mentally withdrawing one of his judgments. But either kind of correction involves events in time, if only a change of mind by the subject of experience.

It has been questioned, however, whether the possibility of detection and correction follows from the mere possibility of being incorrect in any one case. To give meaning to the latter, is it not enough for it to be true of the subject that he could have judged differently, or would have done so if things had been otherwise?[25] But now the problem is how on earth one could understand, let alone have evidence for, such modal and counterfactual statements in the supposed absence of any possibility of change. It is hard indeed to see how in an atemporal experience there can be any distinction between actuality and potentiality. Appeal may however be attempted to generalization over spatially distinct cases, as a basis for a counterfactual judgment about non-temporal experience: for instance, taking stock of a complex visual field, one might note that one judges this blob and that one to be circular, and decide therefore that one would judge that third patch to be circular too, were it not noticeably elongated into the ellipse one actually judges it to be.[26]

The Temporality of Experience

This is the extreme to which the suggestion of non-temporal experience leads us. It seems strange indeed, but can we <u>show</u> it to be absurd?[27] There are several points inviting attack. We may question the very possibility of purely private judgment, where the time-consuming process of communication of others' judgments is ruled out - and at a later stage (4.32) we will be doing just that. We may well wonder whether the sort of second-order mental functioning in the story just told - the reviewing of first-order judgments, the formulation of generalizations about them, and the drawing of counterfactual conclusions - must not itself take place in time. Is there not a directing of attention, <u>first</u> to one aspect, <u>then</u> to another, of one's supposedly unchanging experience? The suggestion of an infinite mind, who can simultaneously (or rather, non-temporally) contain (if not perform) all these mental states (if not acts) is very difficult to make any sense of, but hard to prove logically impossible.[28] The most direct blow seems to be to insist on what is implied by the possibility of mistake, which it is admitted on all sides is essential to judgment.[29] How can the notion of correct and incorrect judgment make sense unless the notion of <u>changing</u> one's judgment also does? And how can counterfactual statements about judgings make sense unless there <u>can</u> be change in the relevant mental acts?[30]

If it is thus possible to change one's mind on any particular question, we must be able to distinguish this from simply changing the subject-matter, making another judgment on a different topic. Having first judged that <u>p</u>, there must be a difference between later judging that <u>not-p</u> and making the logically independent judgment that <u>q</u>. We therefore require a traditional notion of proposition, as something which can be the content or target of two or more temporally distinct acts of judgment. Nothing yet said requires there to be change in the topics of (first-order) judgments, i.e. change in the sensory content of experience, as opposed to change of the topics of judgment. If one first judges that p, and then that q, it does not follow that the world has changed, it may be only that one has directed one's attention to a different aspect of things. Thus we have so far shown the need only for potential change of judgments, not yet for change in the states of affairs judged about.

The truth-value of propositions, the objects of our temporal acts of judgment, is timeless; despite whatever change there may be in the world, propositions by definition remain eternally true or false, and one and the same proposition can at any time be judged, rightly or wrongly, to be true.[31] The necessary truth that human reason has in this sense the power to transcend its position in time, and the mutability of everything material, has been made much of in metaphysics.[32] Our argument here has been that even if there were no change in the world, the very notion of judging requires the possibility of change of mind on the part of the judger. Time is the form of understanding.[33]

Chapter Three

THE LOGICAL FORMS OF JUDGMENTS

Let us now concentrate on the feature that experience, in our sense, involves the making of judgments, and try to unpack in more detail what this implies. We will have to distinguish several different ways in which the term 'judgment' may be used, select the meaning we intend, and analyse what it involves.

3.1 THOUGHT WITHOUT LANGUAGE

When a cat lurks patiently outside a mouse-hole, ignoring human attempts at distraction, we very naturally attribute to her the belief that a mouse is likely to emerge, and we do so all the more willingly if we know that she is hungry and has recently seen mice entering the wainscot. When a dog jumps up with every appearance of eager anticipation whenever its master puts on his coat, it becomes almost irresistible to ascribe to him (the dog, that is) the thought that he is about to be taken for a walk. In a nation of animal-lovers, far be it from me to suggest that such employments of the terms 'belief' and 'thought', or the related applications of 'judgment' or 'concept', are misuses of the English language. It may be that the curious pleasure that most of us seem to derive from such conceptual interpretations of the behaviour of our household pets (and of our pre-linguistic infants) leads us, at least sometimes, into an anthropomorphism which is unjustified by the strict canons of scientific objectivity - note, for example, how easily words like 'patiently' and 'eager' creep

17

into the very description of the evidence above. But even ethologists observing the behaviour of animals in the wild, and deliberately resisting any temptation to treat them as honorary members of their household, seem to find it impossible adequately to explain the doings of lions, dolphins, or chimpanzees without ascribing to them some perceptual beliefs, memories of particular facts, and expectations and plans for the immediate future.

It would be over-zealous, then, for the philosopher to attempt to ban such ascription of propositional attitudes to dumb creatures. It is more enlightening (for philosophers, biologists, and pet-lovers alike) to ask what distinguishes "higher" creatures from others in this respect, what exactly it is that we can do that they cannot, and whether there are (or can be) intermediate levels of ability between them and us supposedly superior beings. Of course, the use of language makes an enormous difference, but what precisely counts as language-use, and is it one integrated ability, or a possibly separable cluster of them?

3.11 Judgments without Language

Firstly, what justifies the ascription of judgments (in one sense of the term) to dogs and cats, lions and chimps, but not, presumably, to worms or spiders? The latter have desires or wants, or at least needs which they can satisfy by appropriate behaviour, in circumstances perceptible to them. Some of them can learn from experience, in the sense that need-satisfying responses are made with much-increased frequency after exposure to stimuli regularly associated with reward or the reverse. (Birds apparently can learn to shun one kind of caterpillar and gobble another). But such capacity to acquire stimulus-response connections hardly seems enough even for our most minimal sense of judgment. What marks out some at least of the mammals for this honour would seem to be a certain complexity of connection, in that the response is made not with automatic regularity but depending on present desires, and not just to one simple kind of perceptual stimulus but to situations which are relevantly similar although perceptually different. For example, the dog may go through his "walk-anticipating" performance not in every case of seeing his master's coat - not, perhaps, when he has just come back from a long outing or when he has just consumed an enormous meal; and he may jump up with equal alacrity when, in summer-time, his master forgoes all outer apparel and takes only a stick, or teasingly utters 'Walkies!' without stirring from the armchair. It is surely this kind of complexity and modifiability of connection between stimulus and response that makes the relevant distinction; once we have seen this, we may if we wish, use the previously vague terms 'intelligence' or 'judgment' to mark it.[34]

3.12 Conditions for Symbol-Use

The next question is what difference does language make? But this should make us ask what counts as language. No behaviour deserves description as the use of symbols or language unless it can be explained as performed in order to communicate something. Regularity of stimulus-response association, even of a complex kind, may be necessary for language but it hardly seems sufficient. To describe the dog's excited yelps as expressing his anticipation of a walk is not to imply that he thereby means to say that he expects a walk.

Ascription of this latter kind of intention requires at least that the creature's intelligence can be seen to be applied to the relation between its supposedly communicative behaviour and its perceived opportunities for achieving satisfaction thereby.[35] But is this enough? If our cat miaows when she is hungry, and sees someone in the room, and smells food, but not when only one or two of these conditions hold, it seems hard not to "get the message" that she wants you to give her the food she knows is there. Yet to ascribe this <u>meaning</u> to her sound is not justified, for she may miaow just the same way when she wants to be let out and sees you near the door. If she develops different kinds of miaow for the two types of need, then we may be tempted to credit her with symbolic behaviour. But this is hardly enough, for each could be described as a learned response to the conjunctions hunger/person/food-smells and full bladder/person/front door; and even if she can learn to use her two sounds upstairs, well away from kitchen and garden, to indicate her needs, that could still be explained by dropping the third member from these trios.

What further kind of complexity is involved in symbolic behaviour? If some kind of noise <u>n</u> (or other performance) is to count as meaningful for a creature <u>c</u>, the ascription of meaning to <u>n</u> for <u>c</u> must play a non-redundant role in the explanation of <u>c</u>'s utterances of <u>n</u>, or responses to <u>n</u>; that is, those utterances or responses must <u>not</u> be explicable just as learned responses to some standard perceptual stimulus. Meaning, belief, and desire must each give an independent contribution to the explanation. For example, if a dog who has been trained to obey some standard commands then develops the independence of spirit to comply only when he can see that the speaker is in a position to punish disobedience, or to bribe him with food, then it seems reasonable to ascribe understanding of those words of command. The proud mother's claim that her infant has just enounced his first word (and meant it) can be vindicated only if the little prodigy not only comes out with the same phonemes in similar perceptual situations, but can use them, or react to them, in other appropriate circumstances too – for example, if on hearing the word, he will search around for the object it denotes and display it for parental congratulation on his cognitive achievement.

3.2 **A PRIMITIVE LANGUAGE**

Now that we have a clearer conception of what must be involved in any behaviour that is to count as linguistic use or understanding, we can focus on the necessary conditions for assertion. This should be a help towards exploring the necessary conditions for judgment, in the sense involved in our longer-term aim.

3.21 **Assertion and Denial**

Suppose then that we have a creature capable of assertions. What can they be about, and what form can they take? Some of them must be about situations which are presently perceptible to the creature, for the notion of perceptual belief, along with that of desire to communicate, is (we have argued in 1.13 as well as 3.12) one that we must simultaneously be applying if the ascription of assertion is to have any genuine explanatory value. Now any assertion must have a specific content, it must be an assertion that p, rather than something is the case. What makes it true that an utterance has whatever content it has? Clearly, there must be some connection between utterances of the noise and the kind of perceptual situations in which they are made. But what sort of connection? Of course, we intuitively want to say that the assertion is true, or at least justified, in some situations and not others; that is, there is some standard or rule by which some acts of assertion are correct and other (actual or possible) acts incorrect.[36]

We shall be pondering deeper implications of this in 4; the point to be made here arises from the fact that the assertor himself must be able to manifest some disposition to adjust his assertive acts to meet relevant standards or rules, for otherwise nothing makes it the case that he is asserting, rather than emitting sound-patterns in certain regular, causally explicable ways. Withdrawal of an assertion in the face of new evidence – a better view of the relevant situation, perhaps – would of course manifest the required disposition. But how are we to recognize what constitutes withdrawal, evidencing a change of mind? There needs to be some symbol, or some behaviour anyway, which is interpretable as negating an assertion, or at least as expressing dissent from it. Even if our creature were never to make a mistaken assertion, and thus never need to exercise sufficient humility to take back something he has said, still if he is making assertions at all, he must have the capacity deliberately to refuse to make an assertion when he lacks the appropriate perceptual belief. But there must be a difference between this refusal to assert, and the mere absence of assertion – which may be due to unwillingness to communicate, or inattention, confusion, or sleep. Deliberate silence is, in relevant situations, as significant as utterance; it is not at all the same thing as total lack of response.

Thus the ascription of assertion implies the speaker's capacity to distinguish, for any one of the sentences in his repertoire, between the situations in which it is correctly assertible and those in which it is <u>not</u> thus warranted. Such a capacity can be manifested in appropriate use of a symbol (which we will naturally interpret as 'No!') or by a gesture such as a shake of the head, or at the very least by the kind of significant silence or immobility which is interpretable as intelligent dissent.

What we are saying is that anyone capable of assertion or assent, must be equally capable of denial or dissent. He does not have to have a negating-symbol in his language, but he has the capacity for use of such a symbol; to add it to his vocabulary involves no conceptual advance for him. We should be careful, though, about reading too much into the term 'negation' here. All it imports so far is dissent from an assertion; it has not yet been construed as the assertion of something else instead (<u>the</u> negation of the proposition). That is, any so-called "negation symbol" concatenated with $\underline{p}$ will mean "the assertion of $\underline{p}$ is not now warranted" rather than "$\underline{p}$ is false", for we have not yet found a use for a concept of <u>falsity</u>, any more than for truth as distinct from warranted assertibility.

How can we interpret a symbol or gesture as expressing dissent from assertions? Clearly, there needs to be a recurring kind of noise or movement which can be concatenated or associated with any assertion in the repertoire. And we expect the speaker to be prepared (if willing to co-operate at all) to assent or dissent, but not both at once, to any such assertion.

3.22 Conjunction

It is not credible that there could be the capacity to make just one assertion. As noted, there must be the ability to distinguish when an assertion is warranted from when it is not; and if there is that skill, is there not an ability to distinguish perceptual situations <u>within</u> the latter class? If, for example, a child can recognize red, can he not also distinguish some other colours within the class of situations not warranting the utterance of 'Red!'? And given someone capable of various assertions, surely he can assert conjunctions ($\underline{p}$ and $\underline{q}$) - for if he knows when $\underline{p}$ is warranted, and when $\underline{q}$ is, presumably he <u>a fortiori</u> knows when the conjunctive assertion is warranted, namely when both conditions are simultaneously satisfied.

However, it is not obvious that any assertor must have a <u>symbol</u> meaning 'and'. It seems that only in the presence of other kinds of connection between assertions will such a symbol begin to do any real work. Given an 'if ... then' connective with <u>modus ponens</u> as its rule of inference, one can recognize inferences of the form: If ($\underline{p}$ and $\underline{q}$) then $\underline{r}$; ($\underline{p}$ and $\underline{q}$); <u>ergo</u> $\underline{r}$ as validated by the rule provided one can recognize ($\underline{p}$ and $\underline{q}$) as a unit, an assertion of a conjunction rather than just a conjunction of assertions. Again, if there is in the language some way of expressing generality, perhaps 'Whenever $\underline{p}$ then $\underline{q}$', then there is point in distinguishing ($\underline{p}$ and not-$\underline{q}$) as a counter-example to a general assertion, for the latter excludes neither p nor not-q separately, only their conjunction.

But although in the absence of conditionality or generality, a symbol meaning 'and' is not necessary, it is not ruled out; adding it to the language hardly seems a new conceptual step (it might function as a device for stringing a series of assertions together, to keep the attention of one's hearer, or to discourage him from interrupting). Once negation and conjunction are in the language, some form of propositional logic becomes applicable - but the speaker need not be aware of this possibility, of course.[37]

3.23 Feature–placing Language

It seems that there could be a creature (or artefact) capable of a certain range of assertions, using symbols for negation and conjunction to connect them, but having no concept of conditionality (except in a purely truth-functional sense) and none of generality. Such a being would have no symbols meaning 'if', 'every', 'some', 'whenever', or 'sometimes'. Empirical investigation can tell us whether there is a distinguishable stage of child–development deserving this description, and whether chimpanzees can learn this much symbol–use.

But we should realize the depth of the logical gulf (or the height of the cliff) which lies between this and the language which we (rational beings as we take ourselves to be) are familiar with in our daily intercourse. For one thing, there is nothing in the behaviour of our primitive language–user to require us to interpret his assertions as being in any <u>tense</u> other than the present. In order to ascribe both past and present tense to his conceptual equipment, we would need to find some feature of his symbolic repertoire which was used in such a way as to make the distinction between 'p̲ now' and 'it has been the case that p̲'. But, for all that has been said so far about his performance, it may be perfectly possible to interpret his every assertion as about his present perceptual situation, and unreasonable to attribute any temporal concepts to him.

For another thing, there need be nothing in his behaviour which leads us to discern any internal structure in his assertions (except perhaps that due to his use of negation and conjunction). There need be no division, with any meaning for him, of his utterances into subject and predicate, singular term and general term, or referring phrase and description. Of course we can begin to describe the sort of linguistic use in perceptual context which would motivate such subdivision (and we shall do so in the next section), but the present point is that there could be a language-game which consisted in nothing more than assertions about presently-perceived states of affairs within which no significant structure was discerned. The sentences would be syntactically and semantically simple ("one-word observation sentences"), even if phonetically complex. Perhaps children go through a stage at which they can reliably utter single words of English, such as 'red', 'hot', 'water', 'sugar', 'mama', 'dada', 'cat', 'bird', etc., in response to the appropriate perception, but without joining words into sentences or doing anything else to suggest that they understand the semantic differences between adjectives, mass terms, proper names, and sortal terms.[38] If so, their utterances could at that stage be construed only as one-word observation sentences (which we might attempt to represent in our adult language as of the form 'There is something present to which the word ... applies'). In this sense, such a language may be called "feature-placing".[39]

Provided we recognize the clear differences between this level of linguistic achievement and, on the one hand, behaviour as mentioned in 3.1 involving no symbol-use at all, and on the other, the fully-fledged tensed and generalizing use we are about to examine in 3.3, then it is merely a terminological decision where we apply the words 'judgment', 'language', 'intelligence', 'concepts', 'rationality', etc. It may well be that the pre-theoretical use of these terms does not clearly determine how we should apply them in an inquiry such as this, and can thus give rise to disputes which are fruitless because merely verbal.

3.3 LANGUAGE IN THE FULL SENSE

We now concentrate on what is involved in language and judgment in what I have just called the fully-fledged sense. As already hinted, this new level of conceptual sophistication is reached as soon as there is any significant subdivision of sentences, whether into subject and predicate, radical and tense-indicator, or predicates and quantifier-words. But can we show that reference, tense, and generality mutually presuppose each other?

3.31 Generality

One generality-expressing word in a language (e.g. 'every', 'none', 'some', 'whenever', 'never', 'sometimes') is enough, in combination with negation and conjunction, to allow the formulation of the four classic forms of statement dealt with in the ancient theory of the syllogism. When combined with relational expressions, we get the more complex forms of statement (e.g. 'Every $\underline{F}$ is $\underline{R}$ to some $\underline{G}$', etc.), whose semantics requires the modern logic of quantifiers. Not of course that a user of 'every' need possess any ability to theorize about his skill, let alone to cope with the symbols of quantificational logic; it is merely that he has that which is the subject-matter of such second-order discussion.

But what manifests generality in thought or language? What would show that a chimpanzee or infant means to assert that whenever p then q? Obviously, a necessary condition is the making of the relevant inferences: if an utterance is to be interpreted as having this meaning, we expect the speaker, when presented with a situation in which he recognizes that p is assertible, to be prepared to assert q - or, if not, to withdraw the general statement. And, if he is ever to acquire the disposition to make general judgments, we will expect that after repeated exposure to conjunctions of p with q, with no experience of p without q, our speaker may come out with the assertion that whenever p then q. (We need not suppose that he is so research-oriented as to notice every regularity in his experience which is formulable in his vocabulary, but he can hardly be supposed to have got the hang of generality unless he can sometimes acquire general beliefs as well as act on them.)

It needs no further argument, then, to show that generality presupposes singularity, i.e. that someone can make general statements only if he is master of the appropriate singular statements with which, by definition, they are inferentially connected. But, as hinted already by examples, the singular reference can be to times, to occasions of more instantiation of features, just as much as to objects in any more substantial sense of the word. So there could, apparently be an extension to the feature-placing language of 3.2, consisting merely in the addition of the two-place connective 'Whenever ... then ...' without involving any conceptual division of the features, p, q, etc., which it connects. But for a connective to play this role, it would have to interact appropriately with other actors on the intellectual scene, notably with identifications of <u>particular</u> past or present instantiations of features. It is thus required that singularity and tense be there in the language, to allow reference to specific instances (times of occurrence) of p, q, etc., and to past as well as present instances.[40]

3.32 Singular Reference

What is presupposed by the ability to make reference to particular cases? We shall argue that the use of tenses other than the present is required. Two categories of item have been mooted as targets of singular reference: <u>times</u> (or more concretely, occasions of instantiation of general features), and <u>material objects</u> (which, by definition, endure through time). In the first case, to be able now to refer to a past instance surely implies some mastery of a past tense – otherwise what is to distinguish reference to a past occasion from reference to a distant or imaginary one?

In the second case, what makes it the case that a child refers to particular material objects (his mother, or the family cat), rather than merely using the words as general terms, uttering them when confronted with any woman or cat? Of course, the child may narrow down his linguistic responses, saying 'Mama!' and 'Cat!' only when presented with his own mother or cat, but if that were all the evidence we had to go on, it could be most economically explained by an ability to recognize some more complex, but still general, cluster of features which distinguished the relevant mum or puss from others in the child's experience so far. Attributing singular reference is not really required until the terms are used in suitable sentences, and crucially in assertions of identity and non-identity. Mastery of sentences of the form 'This is the same person (or cat, etc.) as ...' conclusively demonstrates comprehension of what a particular object is.[41] But note that the blank has to be fillable by something in the past tense, for the relevant mastery involves recognizing successive appearances of the same individual.[42] The same test is required for use of words like 'woman', 'cat' as terms for sorts of persisting individual substances, rather than mere features with no distinction between 'the same F as before' and 'another F'.

3.33 The Past Tense

We must now face the subtle question of what conditions are necessary for the use of tense, in particular the past tense. When do we know that a child has learnt that skill? Or, to put the point in another way, suppose we wish to add tense to the feature-placing language of 3.2 - what else has to be the case if this is to be possible? Suppose then that, in addition to a repertoire of feature-recognizing assertions p, q, etc., a speaker employs some symbol 'P' in utterances of the form 'Pp', 'Pq', etc. What would make it the case that 'P' has the meaning 'It has been the case that ... '?

Of course, we can easily imagine that our speaker comes out with '$\underline{Pp}$' when and only when he has in the past been sensorily confronted with at least one case of $\underline{p}$. This, or some approximation to it, is obviously a necessary condition for use of a past tense. But it is hardly sufficient, for nothing in this evidence rules out our interpreting '$\underline{P}$' as 'I presently have a memory-impression that ... ', or better (since the very word 'memory' imputes a concept of the past) as 'I have a peculiar kind of thought that ... '. What is to make the assertion one about the <u>past</u>, rather than about the present mental state of the speaker? Even if the relevant mental states should correlate perfectly with past facts (intuitively, no forgetting or misremembering), they cannot constitute the entire conditions for warranted assertion about the past. Unless there is at least the logical possibility of wrong assertion about the past, there is no concept of the past at all.[43]

In particular cases, one can suggest how one may be justified in saying 'I seem to remember that $\underline{p}$, nevertheless $\underline{p}$ was not the case.' To give an example which is apparently within the area of private mental states, I might conclude that I did <u>not</u> actually have a headache yesterday even though I seem to remember having one, on the grounds that my headaches have always been associated with a queasy stomach and I definitely remember the heartiness of my appetite yesterday. Clearly, any argument of this form makes appeal, in order to correct or confirm judgment about the past, to another such judgment and to a <u>generalization</u> which must itself be based on past cases. We have ways of correcting any one doubtful assertion, but no formula for giving assertion-conditions for statements about the past in terms of statements purely about the present. (It would be surprising indeed if if we were to stumble upon something that succeeds where ancient attempts to define time fail.) Probably the most we can hope to achieve by way of philosophical clarification is some account of the structual interrelationships of our temporal concepts. The immediately relevant conclusion here is the holistic one that someone can make one assertion about the past only if he is prepared to make others, and to asert some kind of general statements.

3.34 Conditionality

The ability to make general judgments makes possible the use of condionals in a more than purely truth-functional sense. For, as noted, if someone judges that whenever p then q, we will expect him, in situations where he judges that p, to infer that q. He could therefore have an 'if ... then' connective in his vocabulary, such that for any specification 't' of a particular occasion, he will be prepared to assert 'If p at t, then q at t', even if he does not know that q at, or that not-p at t. The generalization gives him a <u>reason</u> for inferring from one singular judgment to another, and he can say that there <u>is</u> such a reason by use of the propositional connective 'if'.[44]

3.35 Rationality

Looking back over this discussion, in 3.1 we admitted that in a certain sense there can be judgments without language, and in 3.2 we described a primitive use of symbols, to which we were prepared to allot the title 'feature-placing language'. Then in 3.3 we have been arguing that the abilities conspicuously absent from the latter must, if they are present at all, be all

32

present together. In 3.31 we claimed that generality presupposes singularity, in 3.32 that singular reference presupposes tense, and in 3.33 that tense presupposes generality.[45] In 3.34 we also asserted that generality implies the possibility of a non-truth-functional 'if' in statements giving reasons for other statements.

Perhaps then it is not unreasonable, or unhistorical, to use the term 'reason' or 'rationality' to designate this cluster of abilities which, although serially nameable are not (we have argued) separately manifestable.[46] So far as we know, such rationality is confined to the human species (and not even possessed by all of them) - but that of course is an empirical matter. Anyway, when we talk in the rest of this inquiry of "concepts", "judgments", "assertions", or "language" we mean the kind that are involved in this typically human rationality. It is of the powers of "reason" in this sense that we are conducting a critique.

Chapter Four

EMPIRICAL REALISM

Already we have been finding it difficult to hold apart the contributions of sensibility and understanding to experience: any attempt to deduce consequences by concentrating on one and ignoring the other breaks down very soon. So let us take them together as premisses for further inquiry. The state of play is at least this: that any experiencer's states of mind are temporally ordered, and that he makes judgments about the course of his experience. The main point of this section is to confront the question of solipsism, which we have so far kept waiting in the wings. We aim to solve the "Problem of the External World" by showing that solipsistic denial of any distinction between states of the experiencer's mind and states of anything else is ruled out for conceptual reasons. But we will not yet attempt to show anything about materiality or spatiality – we will talk of objective states of affairs rather than objects. If we can show the necessity for there to be some such objective states, that can serve as a premiss for further argument in Chapter 5.

4.1 VARIOUS GRADES OF OBJECTIVE VALIDITY

First it is vital to clarify the relevant notion of objectivity or objective validity. The traditional problem was whether anything can exist unperceived, but we are talking of states of affairs rather than objects, and of judgment rather than mere perception. So our version of the problem would seem to be whether any states of affairs can obtain even if they are not judged to obtain (or, equivalently, whether any propositions can be true although not judged to be true). But it is surely essential to ask: judged by whom, and when? We will now see that if we pay due attention to the relativity of judgment to person and time the issues become more complicated, yet we can with a little care distinguish clearly between various positions that seem prima facie possible.

4.11 Realism, Idealism, Solipsism

For non-mental states of affairs, our ordinary view is that they obtain independently of anyone's judgments about them, i.e. the truth of the relevant propositions neither entails nor is entailed by their being judged to be true by any person. Indeed, we might take this, for the moment at least, as a definition of 'non-mental'. But for states of mind or consciousness there is a difference which has generated clouds of philosophy - smoke-screens of metaphysics, even. For there are ϕ's for which, it seems, A's judging that he is ϕ entails that he is ϕ, although (notoriously) B's judging that A is ϕ does not have this entailment. We need not pause now to determine the exact extension of this class, we may merely note that it is non-empty, for it includes sensations and thoughts, and in fact everything that has gone under the name of cogitatio.[47]

A's being ϕ may, then, be independent of B's judgment, but not of A's. The relevant notion of independence is therefore not a property of propositions (or states of affairs) but a relation. We can clarify this as follows: we shall say that p is independent of a's judgment ('Ipa' for short) if and only if p is neither incorrigible nor self-evident to a; where p is incorrigible to a iff a's judging that p entails that p is true; and

p is self-evident to a iff p's being true and being considered by a together entail that a judges that p.[48]

Equipped with this two-place relation of independence we can now divide the field of possible positions. Realism, in the sense we are concerned with here, is represented by (Ep)(a)Ipa: some proposition is independent of everyone's judgment. This of course entails, but is not entailed by (a)(Ep)Ipa: so it might be that for any given person there is some proposition independent of his judgment (e.g. a proposition about someone else's state of mind), without there being any non-mental states of affairs. This is one kind of idealism.[49] But if even (a)(Ep)Ipa is false, we have (Ea)(p)-Ipa: which we may take as representing solipsism, since it says that there is someone such that no propositions at all are independent of his judgment. The possible positions therefore are:

Realism: (Ep)(a)Ipa
Idealism: -(Ep)(a)Ipa & (a)(Ep)Ipa
Solipsism: -(a) (Ep)Ipa

These three are mutually exclusive (each of them is contrary to both the others) and yet exhaustive (their disjunction is a logical truth).

4.12 Idealism and Solipsism of the Present Moment

But to attain a full understanding of the business in hand, we should take into account the relativity of judgment to time, as well as to person. The notorious non-independence of mental states (their apparent incorrigibility and self-evidence) applies only to present-tense first person judgments about them: A's

36

judging that he is presently ϕ may entail that he <u>is</u> then ϕ, but his judging that he was or will be ϕ does not entail the truth of truth of such past- or future-tense judgments, even though they be about his own mental states. We should recognize therefore that the notion of independence is really a <u>three-</u>place relation between proposition, person, and time, and amend our definitions accordingly. So let us say that <u>p</u> is <u>independent of</u> <u>a</u>'s judgment at time <u>t</u> iff <u>p</u> is neither incorrigible nor self-evident to <u>p</u> at <u>t</u>, that is, iff <u>a</u>'s judging at <u>t</u> that <u>p</u> does not entail <u>p</u>'s truth, and (conversely) <u>p</u>'s truth, together with <u>a</u>'s considering at <u>t</u> whether <u>p</u>, do not entail <u>a</u>'s judging at <u>t</u> that <u>p</u>.

Realism should now be expressed as (E<u>p</u>)(<u>a</u>)(<u>t</u>)<u>Ipat</u>, where '<u>Ipat</u>' represents our three-place relation of independence. Because of the various possibilities of ordering the three quantifiers now involved, we can now distinguish more alternatives to realism. For if (E<u>p</u>)(<u>a</u>)(<u>t</u>)<u>Ipat</u> is denied, we can go on to ask whether the following are denied: (<u>a</u>)(E<u>p</u>)(<u>t</u>)<u>Ipat</u>, which seems to express a realism about other minds at least, for it says that for everyone there is some proposition which is independent of his judgment at any time; and (<u>t</u>)(E<u>p</u>)(<u>a</u>) <u>Ipat</u>, which seems to express a realism at least about past states (even if they should be of one mind only), for it says that at any time there are propositions which are independent of the judgment at that time of whatever minds there happen to be. So <u>five</u> possible positions, mutually exclusive, are:

Realism: (E<u>p</u>)(<u>a</u>)(<u>t</u>)<u>Ipat</u>

Idealism: -(E<u>p</u>)(<u>a</u>)(<u>t</u>)<u>Ipat</u> & (<u>a</u>)(E<u>p</u>)(<u>t</u>)<u>Ipat</u>
                   & (<u>t</u>)(E<u>p</u>)(<u>a</u>)<u>Ipat</u>

Solipsism:	$-(\underline{a})(E\underline{p})(t)\underline{Ipat}$ & $(t)(E\underline{p})(\underline{a})\underline{Ipat}$
Idealism of the present moment:	$(\underline{a})(E\underline{p})(t)\underline{Ipat}$ & $-(t)(E\underline{p})(\underline{a})\underline{Ipat}$
Solipsism of the present moment:	$-(\underline{a})(E\underline{p})(t)\underline{Ipat}$ & $-(t)(E\underline{p})(\underline{a})\underline{Ipat}$

4.2 TIME AND SELF-CONSCIOUSNESS

Our first step should be to exclude solipsism and idealism of the present moment by proving $(\underline{t})(E\underline{p})(\underline{a})\underline{Ipat}$. Suppose this were not true - then it would be the case that $(E\underline{t})-(E\underline{p})(\underline{a})\underline{Ipat}$, that is, there would be a time at which there is no proposition which is independent of everyone's judgment at that time. But at any given time, all propositions about previous states of affairs (whether mental or non-mental) are independent of anyone's judgment at the time, so our supposition implies that there would be no judgments about the past.

Now in 3.3 we have already said that the sense of 'judgment' we are concerned with in this study is that which includes the potential for past-tense judgments, so it may seem that our desired result follows immediately. But is it open to someone enamoured of metaphysical speculations to say that this is mere stipulation of our subject-matter, which does nothing to show the impossibility of a kind of experience and judgment involving no thought of the past? What of him who avers that only his present experience is real?[50] Well, we should certainly ask him what he means by 'my' and 'present', whether indeed he can attach any meaning to these terms if he professes to be unable to apply the usual contrast with other people and other times. But perhaps he will retreat to saying that he has no use for any distinctions between himself and others, or present and past.[51] What then is he still main-taining - presumably, that there is experience, and judgment about the experience.

But now it seems dubious whether our speculator is left with a coherent position. Of course, in 3.2 we have explored the possibility of a feature-placing language with no use of tense, or of personal pronouns either, but that was explained in terms of the behaviour and environment of the language-user; that is, we were able to give sense to a tenseless kind of experience and judgment only from the third-person point of view, in which we presuppose the external world as usual, including the behaviour of the other creature. But our would-be solipsist has painted himself into his present corner by rejecting the use of all such "outer" concepts, and yet - if he is not reduced to emitting an inarticulate sound - he is still trying to maintain that there is experience and judgment. So he cannot evince as his reasons for this, his observation of the behaviour of someone or something else; yet he is claiming to know that there is experience and judgment, not just that they are possible, and it seems that the only ground he can offer for this is first-person awareness of his own mental states. How then can he deny himself the right to refer to himself and his past states, while still retaining grounds for the knowledge he claims of experience and judgment?

It does not seem possible to claim the sort of a priori knowledge of the existence of experience noted in 1.22 without thereby allowing that there is a subject of the experience, who can refer to himself by the first-person pronoun, who endures through time, and can ascribe to himself various temporally successive experiences. "It must be possible for the 'I think' to acompany all my representations; for otherwise something would be represented in me which could not be thought at all, and that is equivalent to saying that the representation would be impossible, or at least would be nothing to me."[52] "If we were not conscious that what we think is the same as what we thought a moment before, ... the manifold of the representation ... would lack that unity which only consciousness can impart to it."[53] The latter thought connects with our claim in 2.2, that it must be possible to know when one's present act of judgment is a confirmation of something already judged, a contradiction of it (representing a change of mind on the topic), or merely a logically independent judgment on a different topic.

Solipsism and idealism of the present moment are therefore incoherent. He who claims a priori knowledge of the existence of experience and judgment must admit the notion of past states of himself, at least.[54] So, to answer a question left open in 1.22, our starting-point can only be 'I have experience', not 'There is experience'.

4.3 STATES OF AFFAIRS DISTINCT FROM ONESELF

If we have succeeded in showing the logical escape from the present moment, the next step is to find the liberation from the restriction to oneself. We have to show that $(\underline{a})(\mathbf{E}\underline{p})(t)I\underline{p}at$, i.e. that for any subject of experience there are propositions which are independent of his judgment at all times; such propositions cannot therefore be about any of his mental states - they may be about the mental states of others or about states which are not mental at all.

4.31 Past Tense and Generality

In arguing for this, we may take as premiss the result of 4.2 and say, in the first person, "I am conscious of my own existence as determined in time."[55] The question now is what must be the case if this is possible? What is presupposed in use of the past tense? In admitting that judgments about the past are independent of their presently being judged, we mean that the truth of the relevant proposition neither entails nor is entailed by its now being judged to be true. We have thus got a difference between "seeming right" (being judged now) and "being right" (being true): the question is what makes this distinction possible.

In 3.33 we argued that someone can make one singular past-tense judgment only if he can make others, and employ general judgments connecting them, for this seemed to be the only way of making possible the required distinction, for any particular judgment, between its seeming right to him and its being right. But as far as we can see, this bringing to bear of regularities or laws does not in itself require judgments to be about anything other than the mental states of the subject.[56] As noted in 3.33, he could notice a correlation between headaches and queasiness, and use it to make inferences about particular doubtful cases of either. But to do this he must at least make a general judgment of some kind, whether of 'all' or 'most' form - otherwise he has no reason for inferring from one singular judgment to another.

A doubt might be voiced here about whether this appeal to correlations, regularities, or laws (whatever term is preferred) is really essential to the possibility of correcting singular judgments. Is not the mere possibility of preferring a "stronger" to a "weaker" judgment, a more "vivid" memory-impression to a somewhat "faded" one, enough to give meaning to the contrast between seeming and being right?[57] This is an attempt to appeal to some <u>felt quality</u> of acts of judgment, rather than to their <u>content</u> and its logical relation to that of other judgments. As such, it does not in itself provide the right sort of reason for correcting any one judgment, or inhibiting any inclination to believe.[58] Of course, one may find that some such quality <u>correlates</u> with truth, and thereafter come to rely on such vivacity as a mark of reality, but obviously this presupposes an independent criterion of truth or reality. The availability of the relevant sort of reason is essential to any notion of the past, to make the distinction between true memory and vivid memory-impression. Might is not right, in epistemology or elsewhere.

It is tempting to suppose that sufficient regularities will be forthcoming only if experience is such as to justify the application of concepts of present states of affairs distinct from the subject's mental states, but we have still not found any conclusive argument to prove the point.[59] The result can, I suspect, be arrived at only by a yet deeper inquiry into the necessary conditions for judgment.

4.32 Following a Rule

The state of play is that we admit that any experience of which the subject can judge 'I am having experience which is thus-and-so' must be such that he can also make past-tense and general judgments; but we have not yet seen why the topics of such judgments need be anything other than the mental states of the subject (i.e. states whose obtainings are not independent of his present-tense judgments that they obtain). We have already claimed that he cannot know himself to be judging unless he can have some knowledge of his past; now we will argue that he cannot be judging at all unless there is a certain appropriate relation between his (singular) past judgments and his present judgment - a relation expressed in the phrase 'following a rule'.

The point is that any judgment must have some specific content, it must be a judgment that p rather than q; and, as we have previously argued (in 2.2), it must be possible for different acts of judging (made at distinct times) to have the same content. Splitting the 'p' into general feature f and the time t at which, according to the content of 'p', it is supposed to hold, it must be possible for two judgings (at times t_1 and t_2) both to be judgments that f holds at time t_3; it must also be possible for two judgings to be present-tense judgments, made at different times, about f - i.e. judging at t_1 that f holds at t_1, and judging at t_2 that f holds at t_2.[60] The question now is: what gives these judgings their common content? What must be the case if two or more mental acts are to be judgments about the holding of feature f, rather than some other feature?

"Following a rule" is supposed to constitute the answer to these questions - the subject can be said to be judging if and only if he is following some rule or other in his mental acts, and to be judging that p (or that f holds at t) if and only if he is following a certain specific rule.[61] But of course we have so far only a slogan: it remains to be explained what it means, how it constitutes an answer to our questions, and why it leads to the rejection of solipsism.

Firstly, the point must be emphasized that we are at this stage taking a first- rather than third-person point of view; we are not discussing the conditions for ascribing judgments to some creature whose behaviour we are observing, but rather the conditions for any subject of experience to ascribe experience and judgment to <u>himself</u>. Secondly, following a rule does <u>not</u> (in either first- or third-person case) imply that the subject (or the observers of his behaviour) can <u>state</u> the rule he is following in any terms other than those involved in the relevant judgment. We can tell when a child has learnt the standard use of the English words 'red', 'hot', 'water', 'cat', and many others, without our being able to give necessary and sufficient conditions for their application in any terms which do not re-use those very words (we simply check whether the child agrees with us in the application and witholding of the words in a reasonably wide range of samples presented to him in normal perceptual conditions). In the first-person case, if the subject can judge when he feels toothache, queasiness, pleasantly warm, nostalgic for the experiences of yesteryear, or somewhat anxious about those to come, it does not follow that he can offer (even to himself, in his possibly-solipsist state) any explicative judgments about the rules he is following; all that is required is a certain consistency of practice.

The crucial question is what the required "consistency of practice" can and must be. We have already argued that our subject can make, at various times, present-tense judgments about the holding of certain features, and moreover, that he can correct any past-tense judgments (if he doubts his memory) by appealing to generalizations and other singular judgments. Is not this enough to meet our requirements, to allow him to be described as following a rule? We have admitted that it is not possible that there should be only one occasion on which he obeys a rule[62] - there must be a practice, if there is to be consistency of practice. But does it follow that it is not possible to obey a rule "privately"[63] - or could the relevant practice be entirely private, in the solipsistic sense that it would be logically impossible for anyone else to judge whether the subject is following any particular rule , or any rule at all?[64]

Well, suppose this were so. Then the claim is that on each occasion when the subject judges that a given feature f is now present, he can be following a rule so as to make it the case that he is then judging that f rather than g obtains. Now however many judgments he may have made in the past, the question is what makes it now the case that he is (once again or for the first time, carelessly or reflectively, rightly or wrongly, judging that f holds?. At this point, appeal to past cases and generalizations about them cannot help, because it presupposes just what is being questioned, namely whether there is sufficient consistency of practice between past and present mental acts to constitute them as judgments about f.[65] If we imagine our subject using a language to express his judgments, then the question is what makes it the case that he is now using a certain word with a certain meaning - but even if, in our attempt to give the solipsist every inch of rope with which to hang himself, we "think away" the utterance of sounds or any such physical event, the point remains that the analogue of meaning has to be a property of the subject's mental acts, they must have specific content.

Now if it is logically ruled out that anyone else can make a judgment about whether or not $\underline{f}$ presently holds, and communicate their agreement or disagreement about the case, then there is nothing that makes any difference between the protagonist's thinking he is obeying the relevant rule and actually doing so, that is, between his taking himself to be judging that $\underline{f}$ and his really judging thus. For him to be following a rule at all, it must be logically possible that in any given case he fail to follow it. And the relevant kind of failure – not so much making a false judgment, but the mental analogue of forgetting the meaning of a word – makes sense only if it can somehow be presently manifested to the subject. But if his present mental states (including memories of past ones) are all he has to go on, this is not possible. He must therefore accept the logical possibility of others' present judgments being communicated to him.[66] If memory is a source of knowldge, so must testimony be.

Admitting the logical possibility of others' judgments is inconsistent with solipsism, as we have defined it, for we thereby admit that there are states of affairs (concerning other people, at least) such that whether or not they hold at a given time is independent of the judgment of our postulated protagonist at that time, $(E\underline{p})(\underline{t})\underline{I}pat$. And since nothing in our argument depends on any special property of the protagonist, we may generalize about all possible subjects of experience, and assert $(\underline{a})(E\underline{p})(\underline{t})\underline{I}pat$.

4.4 STATES DISTINCT FROM ANYONE'S JUDGMENT

One stage remains, to complete our journey through these metaphysical realms and bring us back to common sense. That step is to exclude idealism and thereby prove realism, in the sense we gave to these over-used terms in 4.12; thus we have to invert the order of quantifiers and find ground to assert not merely $(\underline{a})(E\underline{p})(\underline{t})I\underline{pat}$, but $(E\underline{p})(\underline{a})(\underline{t})I\underline{pat}$.

Fortunately (for those wearied by the conceptual rigours of our transcendental travel) we have acquired enough momentum to cover the last stage easily. The notion of others' judgment, for which, in effect, we have just claimed categorial status (i.e. that in any conceivable experience, it must be possible to apply it) cannot make sense without notions of states of affairs which are not mental. There are two connected reasons for this, to do with the topics of others' judgments and with their communication.

Imagine a group of people who talked about nothing else but each other's mental states:[67] for this to be a true description of their communication we would surely have to suppose it possible (even if not the done thing) for them to discuss the behavioural evidence for their mutual attributions. That is, the idea of a group in which telepathy was the only source of mutual knowledge, and perception impossible, is incoherent. This is not merely because telepathy is presumably knowledge of another's mental states not based on any perception of the body or anything causally dependent on it, and is therefore a notion which can be understood only if we have the ordinary notions of bodies and perception. For suppose someone tries to persuade us of the coherence of idealism by attempting to detach the notions of mental state and telepathy from their normal bodily background, abstracting to a heavenly or angelic state in which we do not even have the resurrected bodies with which orthodoxy provides us, but are disembodied souls. What, in such a condition, would make it the case that any judgment by A is about a mental state of B? What, that is, would be the difference between A's being right about B and its seeming to him that he is right? Telepathy does not require A to have B's mental states (for that, he would have to be B), it means only that A knows about them, i.e. that he is reliably right on the topic. But plainly this implies that there must be some criterion of being right, some test which A's relevant judgments usually pass. So A's judgment, if genuinely about B, must be communicable, and open to evaluation by reference to publicly available facts about B. The possibility of testimony presupposes that of perception.

So our conclusion is that any coherent notion of self-conscious experience must admit both mental states of other people and states of affairs independent of all judgment at all times. Knowledge of one's present mental state presupposes the possibility of knowledge of the past, of other minds, and of the external world. Present-tense avowals stand or fall with memory, testimony, and perception. In Chapter 5 we concentrate on what is implied by the obtaining of material states of affairs, and then in 6 we go on to inquire more closely into the attribution of mental states to oneself and to others.

Chapter Five

THE MATERIAL WORLD

We have shown that any self-conscious experience must involve the acknowledgment of states of affairs which are not states of one's own, or of anyone else's, mind. "Concepts of objects in general thus underlie all empirical knowledge as its a priori conditions."[68] 'Object in general' means for us just any state of affairs whose obtaining is independent of any particular judgment about it; such states include, we shall argue, the properties of persisting material objects, but for all that we have seen so far, they might consist entirely in the holding of various objective features, e.g. heat, rain, sounds, and smells, at certain times.

The next stage of our argument must take into account the fact that our states of mind <u>change</u>. Time, as shown in 2, is the form of sensibility and understanding: there is no conceivable experience which does not involve change in one's judgments. It is thus possible that my judgment at t_1 that objective feature $\underline{f}$ holds at $\underline{t}_1$ is followed by the absence of any judgment at $\underline{t}_2$ about $\underline{f}$ at $\underline{t}_2$. But such a change in my mind does not entail any corresponding change in the world: it is perfectly consistent with $\underline{f}$ still holding at $\underline{t}_2$, for I may have simply directed my attention to something more interesting, or if I judge at $\underline{t}_1$ that $\underline{f}$ obtains at $\underline{t}_1$, and then at $\underline{t}_2$ that it no longer obtains at $\underline{t}_2$, either of these judgments could be wrong. Conversely, change in the world does not entail change in my judgment, for if $\underline{f}$ holds at $\underline{t}_1$ but not at $\underline{t}_2$, I might blissfully ignore the whole topic of f, or if I do venture a judgment on the matter I could be mistaken.

So the time-order of judgments is not the same as the time-order of events, i.e. changes in the objective states of affairs which are the topics of those judgments. "Since experience is a knowledge of objects through perceptions, the relation involved in the existence of the manifold has to be represented in experience, not as it comes juxtaposed in time but as it exists objectively in time."[69] There must therefore be some way in which the subject can draw distinctions between changes in his judgments and changes in the world. The very notion of objectivity implies that we have the conceptual resources to do this. It remains to be seen how it must be done.

5.1 THE PERMANENCE OF THE WORLD AS A WHOLE

If we are to take some of our experiences as perceptions of objective states of affairs, and hence some (but by no means all) of the changes in our perceptions as perceptions of change, we must take the objective events and our perceptions of them as standing in a certain system of relations. A kind of holism is involved here: we can interpret any one experience as a perception of an event only if we are prepared to interpret some other experiences as perceptions of the same event, or related events. There is a faint analogy to the mathematical procedures for answering questions of the form: what quantity b is such that a is to b as b is to c?[70] There is a closer analogy to the holistic explanation of intentional human action in terms of beliefs and desires.[71]

But what sort of system, and what sort of relations, must

be involved here? The first point is that there can be only <u>one</u> such system, that all the events and all the perceptions of them are part of one world. Any particular state of affairs can come to hold, or cease to obtain, and any particular object can come into being, or be destroyed; but all such events are changes in one and the same continuing world. "We require an underlying ground which exists at all times, that is, something abiding and permanent, of which all change and coexistence are only so many ways (modes of time) in which the permanent exists."[72] The system of the world as a whole cannot of course be perceived, it is rather presupposed <u>a priori</u> in taking anything as an objective change.

But <u>must</u> there be only one world-whole? In particular, why only one system of temporal relations? So far, it seems, we have assertion without proof. Let us try, then, to suppose the opposite and see what absurdities we are reduced to. Remember that we are starting from the assumption that one's <u>experiences</u>, at least, fall into a single temporal order.

Does it follow that all the <u>events</u> one experiences are thus related? If I perceive event $\underline{E}$, and then perceive event $\underline{F}$, it need not be that $\underline{E}$ happened before $\underline{F}$ (because of the possibility of time–delays in the perceptual processes), but surely $\underline{E}$ must be <u>either</u> before, simultaneous with, or after $\underline{F}$? Could one coherently take one's temporally ordered experiences as perceptions of objective, but temporally unrelated events?[73] To imagine this, one has to try to transfer the difference between waking and dreaming to a supposed case of two unrelated <u>realities</u>. Or one might imagine a discontinuity in experience like that between sequences in a film, except that they are taken not as different events within one world, but as two or more systems of events between which there are no temporal relations whatsoever.

It seems that any imaginable discontinuity could be accounted for by the former hypothesis rather than the latter. That is, nothing in experience could force us to interpret it as perception of temporally unrelated events, rather than of events within the same world, about whose temporal relationships we were somewhat puzzled (we can always postulate a temporary loss of consciousness). We maintain the unity of time as an a priori truth, simply by not allowing anything to count against it. In practice we discuss certain impressions (however internally coherent) as illusory on the grounds of their total lack of the right sort of connection with everything we count as real. This shows something about the concept of reality - that whatever is to count as real must (like a candidate for acceptance into old-fashioned polite society) be appropriately related to the rest of what we call real. There can be only one system of reality. If we were to start distinguishing different systems unrelated to each other, there would be no reason to treat any of them as real, and no objectivity at all. "The unity of experience would never be possible if we were willing to allow that new worlds could come into existence."[74] (All this has been to do with the unity of time: the need for space, and for its unity, has yet to be explicitly brought out.)

5.2 CAUSALITY, PERCEPTION, AND SPACE

As already shown, change in one's judgments does not entail corresponding change in the world. When one does decide that there has occurred an objective change, this is not implied merely by the temporal order of one's judgments; so there must be some other criterion by which we can know the objective ordering of events. "The objective relation of appearances that follow upon one another is not to be determined through mere perception. In order that this relation be known as determined, the relation between the two states must be so thought that it is thereby determined as necessary which of them must be placed before ... ."[75] We must now explore what can be unpacked a priori about the form any such criterion must take.

5.21 The Need for Spatial Relations

A natural suggestion is that one's judgment as to whether f has just now come to obtain must depend on other features of one's experience at the time, or immediately preceding times. For instance, if one has several times experienced f after feature e, then one has reason, it would seem, to formulate and apply the rule: if one has experience of f at t, shortly after experience e, then f has indeed come into being just then. What could be more rational, and inded more empirical, than to appeal thus to elementary generalizations about what has already occurred within one's experience? The only a priori principle would be that one must rely on such empirically established constant conjunctions of experiences.[76]

But however plausible this classical empiricist suggestion may seem, it is surely somewhat misdirected in the present state of the argument. Induction from previously experienced regularities must certainly have a valid part to play in the total drama, but there are some scenes to be played before its cue comes up. For how can associations within experience give us any reason to infer beyond our present experience, unless we were already able to interpret the past experiences as of objective states and changes? The character of past experience cannot define the meaning of what it is to infer beyond present experience.[77]

We are still searching, then, for criteria by which to distinguish the order of experiences from the objective time-order of happenings. We need to be able to tell the case in which $\underline{f}$ has actually come about from the rest of those in which $\underline{f}$ at least seems to have swum into one's ken, and to distinguish the situation in which $\underline{f}$ is still true but no longer perceived from that in which it no longer holds. How can we do this unless we know a priori that whether or not we seem to perceive $\underline{f}$ (or, "have an experience as of $\underline{f}$") depends in some systematic way on something about $\underline{f}$ itself? We have just been searching for conditions to do with experiences as of $\underline{f}$, but it seemed that we were looking in the wrong place - and the suggestion of the previous sentence is that we should focus our attention on the fact, rather than on the experience of it. Remember that we are not, at this stage, trying to prove the necessity of accepting that states of affairs can hold unperceived; that is supposed to have been shown already, in 4. We are asking, rather, what is implied by this necessity; in particular, how can one apply the idea of states beyond one's present experience? We are therefore entitled to focus on the nature of the objective facts, the existence of which we hope has been sufficiently demonstrated.

What is involved, then, in the notions of $\underline{f}$ seeming to come about without actually doing so, and of $\underline{f}$ holding at $\underline{t}$ although not being perceived then? Certainly, one may have experienced f (and perhaps associated features) already, and one may perceive them again subsequently: but we must remember here the distinction between another instance of f (with similar associated features) and perceiving the same case again. This difference between qualitative and numerical identity is clearest for familiar sorts of material object, but at this stage we are still talking only of objective states of affairs, so let us ask whether any such distinction can be made for features such as rain, sounds, and smells. What could it be to perceive the same instance of rain or sound twice, not merely the same kind of rain or sound? Whatever answers this question will surely also explain what it is for the same rain or sound to be going on unperceived.[78]

Very likely it would be unhelpful for us to inquire too closely into the conditions in which we actually speak of perceiving the same rain or the same sound; the complexities and vaguenesses of ordinary usage here are hardly relevant to our very abstract investigation. But one thing stands out a mile - if one may thus spatially express it - namely, the relevance of place. In so far as it makes any sense to talk of re-identifying the same case or instance of a previously observed feature, it must have been somewhere meanwhile. It must have been instantiated, not merely throughout the relevant time-interval (although not observed continuously through it) but at some position in space, or at least in a continuous series of neighbouring positions. (Even if we talk of the same rainstorm, or the same roadwork-noise, manifesting itself intermittently, the numerical identity surely depends on the spatial continuity of the material source.)

Jumping back to our high level of abstraction, it seems

that the very least that is needed to make conceptually possible the unperceived obtaining of a feature f at time t, is some further indexation or relativization of the obtaining of f at t. Let us label the relevant parameter 's', and talk of f obtaining at s at t. This makes possible a similar relativization of the way in which perceptual experience as of f depends on f's actually holding. In fact, we can now formulate a general principle: <u>If f obtains at s at t, and one is suitably related to s at t, then one seems to perceive f at t.</u>[79] Obviously, the natural substituends for 's' are terms for places in our familiar three-dimensional space, but the formula is general enough to cover various more or less remote analogues of this, such as "places" in a purely auditory world of one dimension, ordered in some systematic but purely auditory way.[80] The important general point is that the notion of perceiving an objective fact implies the <u>law-like</u> dependence of one's perceptual experience, not only on the fact itself, but on one's <u>spatial relation</u> to it. The categorial status of perception involves similar status for causality and space.

5.22 **Material Objects**

Space, and places within it, are not objects of perception, any more than time, or times. We can only witness events occurring <u>at</u> times: we can only perceive things or features <u>at</u> places. The "determination" of an event in time, that is, the judgment as to <u>the</u> time of its occurrence, cannot consist in anything else but specification of its temporal relationships to other events; the unity of time, discussed in 5.1, requires a <u>single</u> system of such relationships. We commonly appeal to a dating system of years and days which depends on regularly recurring events which are especially pervasive, being perceptible to everyone within almost all of the environment in which we conduct our lives. The determination of the place of an event, and of the present location of a thing or feature, must similarly specify its spatial relations to other generally perceptible things in the spatial system. The question now is, what can these be?

Up till now, we have been careful to allow that objective states of affairs can consist in the obtaining of a type of recognizable _feature_ (such as those traditional topics of English conversation – rain, snow, cold, wind, and occasionally, warmth and sunshine) just as much as in the possession of an attribute by a philosophically traditional object or substance. But even these non-substantial yet objective features must, we have argued, occur at specifiable times and places. Our question is, how can their places be specified? Could this be by their spatial relation to other instantiations of features? – but those instantiations can of course be identified only by _their_ place and time, so we are launched on a regress when we ask how _these_ places are to be identified. Obviously, the regress can be stopped, in one way at least, by demonstrative identification – when one says 'Here' and 'Now'. But in so far as this works, it does so only for a hearer who is in the same place as, or at least within earshot of, the speaker. And speaker and hearer themselves must presumably have material bodies: _they_ can hardly be mere instantiations of features.

What exactly does the addition of material objects do to a world of features? Objects have (to put it vaguely at first) a very much more definite sort of identity: they can (in some cases anyway, such as human faces) be very readily recognized as the same particular object - not merely the same sort or type - after many and long absences. But it might be suggested that this is a contingent matter, that there is no logical bar to features, and our discriminations of them, becoming so complex and subtle that we could perceptually recognize _particular_ instantiations - as opposed to new instantiations of the same type - with as much confidence and justification as we now enjoy in personal recognition. Supposing rainstorms to become considerably more long-lasting, mobile, and qualitatively various than they are, and exaggerating the British obsession with the weather to the point of absurdity, we might become personally acquainted with individual rainstorms. (After all, in America, where everything is bigger, they give names to hurricanes.) However, we should realize that this little flight of fancy succeeds only by covertly making a rainstorm into something very like a material object, in the crucial respect of being _mobile_, which surely implies being observable as moving, and hence perceptually _discriminable_ from a relatively static background.

In general, if we are to free instantiations of features from being conceptually tied down to one time and place, and allow them to move around and appear elsewhere, while still being re-identifiable as the same particular instantiation, then we must give a sense to such re-identifications by specifying a criterion of numerical identity. So there must be a way of distinguishing between $\underline{f}$ at $\underline{s}_2$ at $\underline{t}_2$ being the same f-instantiation as was at $\underline{s}_1$ at $\underline{t}_1$, and being merely another case of the general type $\underline{f}$ (e.g. the same rainstorm, not just more rain). What else can this criterion be than the observation of $\underline{f}$

at s_1 moving to s_2 in the interval t_1 to t_2? But such observability requires the particular f-feature to be discriminable from everything else perceived at t_1, at t_2, and in between. This requires the instantiation of the feature to have some intrinsic nature, some form and content to distinguish it from its perceptual background.[81]

If we can perceive movement, there must be a certain system of spatial relations within the relevant sensory modality, as there is in our human senses - most obviously in sight, but also in touch and (less necessarily?) in sound. Our concept of a material object involves, at least as the central cases, the integration of sight and touch; and if the argument forthcoming in 6.12 is correct, tangibility - or some means by which objects can be deliberately manipulated by us - will be in the indispensable core of the concept, even though once we have acquired that core, we may be willing to extend the title to clouds, stars, and atoms. But it is not our business here to examine the empirical details of the sensory modalities of the human species; we are concerned only with the conceptually necessary conditions for experience of objective states of affairs standing in spatial relations. The notion of the perception of movement is enough to give us the concept of something moving, of a substance which persists through time and which can be re-identified as numerically the same despite having changed some or all of its spatial relations to other things.

We thus have a transcendental deduction of the a priori applicability of at least a central part of the concept of material object, namely the concept of a persisting, moveable, re-identifiable individual which can affect one's senses and be affected by one's actions. But nothing in this requires any such object to be sempiternal - neither creatable nor destructible. We commonly accept that many familiar sorts of things begin and cease to be, and when they do, we feel entitled to ask not only when and where the creation or destruction took place, but where the relevant matter came from and what became of it: operating some inchoate conservation principle, we believe there <u>must</u> be answers to such questions. Just what form the conservation principle(s) should take would seem to be a question for physics rather than metaphysics: the recent change from matter to mass/energy may not be the last word on the subject. The only background which seems conceptually required as absolutely permanent is the whole material world, as argued in 5.1.[82]

5.3 THE UNITY OF SPACE

We have argued for a system of spatial relations between the objects and states of affairs in the world, and that all events in the world, all changes in these objects and states, must be temporally related to each other. Does it follow that there must be only one system of spatial relations, i.e. that any object must be spatially related to any other? It is hard indeed to imagine how this could not be so, but "hard to imagine" is often only a challenge to which ingenious philosophers delight to rise, and in this case we do not lack assertions of the unity of time conjoined with denials of the necessary unity of space.[83]

The tall stories which we are invited to accept as cases of two unrelated spaces depend essentially on exploiting the possibility of one's dreams becoming very much more coherent, not only within themselves, but with successive dreams on many nights and with the dream-reports of others, so much so that we are supposed to take the "world" thus experienced as just as real as that of waking life. As with time, we might also think of the cinema, and ask whether we could ever have reason to take a discontinuity in experience like that between sequences in a film as experiences of spatially unrelated things. We have to leap from the contrast between dream and reality, or between two fictions, to one between two spatial realities.

As in 5.1, there seems to be nothing which can <u>force</u> us to make this conceptual jump, for however discontinuous experience might be, we could always say that the things experienced stood in spatial relations of which we were ignorant. But our philosophers' myths are supposed to show that in certain conceivable situations this refusal to jump would be irrational, deserving of the scorn reserved for those who persistently refuse to try. Can we show that the bar is set too high, beyond the logical limits of possible experience?

One ground for thinking so is connected with personal identity, for we are invited to imagine <u>one</u> person experiencing two spatially unrelated realities. There is no question, then, of his body <u>travelling</u> between the locations of observation, so no criterion of personal identity in terms of spatio-temporal continuity of the body can apply: if we accept his claim that <u>he</u> witnessed something spatially unrelated to our here and now, we must simply take his word for it, accepting his assertions as true memory-reports rather than dreams, fictions, or sincerely mistaken memory-impressions. The point is just the same if it is one's own memory-impressions that are in question. The difficulty about this, familiar by now since it crops up at so many stages of our inquiry, is that no perception or memory-impression is self-guaranteeing; seeming to be right is not the same as being right. Any claim to witness another spatial world must be open to evidence for or against it, evidence which consists in something else than the present impressions of one person.

But what if the claims are supported by many people? What if, as the proposed stories suggest, the "dream-world" becomes public in the sense that we not only agree about many of its contents, but can in the here and now recognize causes and effects of it? For instance, we may arrange to meet in the dream and, apparently, keep the appointment; and insults in the dream may leave resentments in the waking world. Would we not then have to take the "dream-world" seriously, reckoning the consequences, for one world, of action in the other?

We need, however, to distinguish between psychological and physical causation here. In the postulated situation of shared and recurring dreams, we might have to be more careful about what we say to people, because this might affect the contents of their dreams, and have repercussions for our subsequent relationships. But this shows only the reality of the dreaming as mental processes within this world, not the truth of the dream-contents in another world. Directly physical effects of dreamed-of "events" would present us with more serious problems, in more ways than one. What if nightmarish accidents caused tangible injuries, or dreamed-of lovemaking produced real-life pregnancies? By an ancient criterion for reality,[84] to describe the situation in these ways would already be to admit the dreams as real, since they have real "effects". But obviously, the "dream-world" and real world are not now unrelated, for we have allowed causality between them, and not merely concerning people's mental states.

We are agreed, then, that any two real things or events must stand in the possibility of causal interaction. "All substances, so far as they coexist, stand in thoroughgoing community, that is, in mutual interaction."[85] But does this exclude the idea of spatially unrelated things – could causation not leap the metaphysical gap, as it were? We have to look more closely at how any such causal relations could be established. It is surely not enough for people to believe in them, otherwise the pop-star of the day could find himself the object of innumerable paternity-suits, and – if the beliefs of juries and judges are decisive – losing them. At the very least, the plaintiff would have to show that the defendant had (in another world) been in sufficiently intimate spatial relation to her. But (we will be told) there could be impressively unanimous testimony to this from regular denizens of the other place when hauled in to court here.

However, there must surely be conceptual problems about the mysterious transitions between worlds which such citizens, like habitual air-travellers, are supposed to get used to. We can hardly suppose that they leave their bodies behind whenever they take their metaphysical trips, for then contradictions quickly develop – how, for example, can a girl lose her virginity in one world while retaining it in the other? We presumably have to suppose that departure and return coincides with disappearance and reappearance of the body, as witnessed by those who stay behind: we cannot allow anything to be in two different places at the same time. Such hiatuses would play havoc with our physics, not to mention our social life (we would have to reckon with the constant possibility of anyone's disappearance, and of them reappearing unpredictably in the most inconvenient situations). If people can thus disappear, why not inanimate objects? After all, are we not allowed to take our clothes, our spectacles, or our false teeth with us? But if there is no limit to what can take these metaphysical leaps, it becomes far from clear whether we are left with a stable enough background on either side to constitute a world: without spatio-temporal continuity as a ground for the identity of objects, how can we apply any concepts of space, time, and objective states of affairs?

"Taken together, the results of Chapter 5 thus declare that all appearances lie, and must lie, in one nature, because without this a priori unity no unity of experience, and therefore no determination of objects in it, would be possible."[86]

Chapter Six

THE MENTAL

If our transcendental deduction in 4 is valid, it provides a solution to scepticism about other minds in the course of answering scepticism about the external world. In 5 we tried to analyse the structure of a priori concepts and principles involved in the notion of objective material states of affairs; now we need to do some unpacking of the a priori elements in the notion of mental states.

6.1 KNOWLEDGE OF OTHER MINDS

In 4.3 we argued that one can have a concept of oneself as a subject of experience only if one allows that others are also capable of judgment. Let us now examine in more detail what must be involved in the third-person ascription of mental states.

6.11 The Judgments and Perceptions of Others

Why must we be able to ascribe judgments to others? Let us rehearse the reasons. Suppose we take as premiss that I can make perceptual judgments about material states; then since I am making judgments, I am following rules in my utterances or mental acts, and there can be rules only if, in any given case, there can be disagreement. It must therefore be possible (as argued in 4.32) for someone else to perceive the state of affairs that is the topic of my judgment, but to make a different, incompatible, judgment about it.

Even if we start (as we did in 4) from my judgments about my own present experience, where the possibility of error is ruled out, there must be a rule that I am following, if I am judging at all. But, once again, there can be a rule only if there can be agreement about its application in a number of cases, and correction of particular misapplications. My own memory-impressions cannot guarantee my agreement with myself over various past cases, so it must be possible for the judgments of others to set the standard to which my present judgment is responsible, if it is to be a judgment at all and to have the specific content it has. So others must be able to make judgments about my present mental states. Otherwise they could never have taught me the meaning of any words for mental states, and could not determine whether I am continuing to use those words with the same meaning. My own inner processes stand in need of outer criteria;[87] and what else can such criteria consist in but facts about my behaviour (and circumstances) which are perceivable by others?

Thus we see the reciprocal dependence between concepts of my own mental states and of the mental states of others. I can ascribe judgments and perceptions to myself only if I can ascribe them to others, and if others can ascribe them to me. Of course this does not rule out the possibility of my being the sole survivor of a nuclear catastrophe, nor perhaps – though this is much less clear – may it exclude my having grown up and learnt everything I know on the proverbial desert island; the point is that nobody can be credited with the concept of himself as one subject of experience unless he recognizes at least the possibility of there being others. Those others have to be understood as embodied beings, occupying positions in space, standing in such causal relations to things as to count as perceivers, and capable of such rule-following behaviour as to count as the authors of judgments.

6.12 The Actions and Desires of Others

In 5.21 we claimed that the notion of objective states of affairs and events requires the a priori truth of the general principle: if f obtains at s at t, and one is suitably spatially related to s at t, then one has perceptual experience of f at t. The appropriate relation involves both one's spatial relation to s (one needs to be at the relevant place, or at least within appropriate perceptual range of it) and the disposition of one's sense-organs (e.g. eyes open and looking in the right direction, or hand extended to touch the relevant object); besides, the relevant perceptual mechanisms need to be in normal working order. Normally, of course, the first two of these are to some considerable extent under one's control: one can, at will, move into perceptual range of a hitherto unperceived state of affairs, and put one's limbs and/or sense-organs into such relation to the object or state that, short of some extraordinary malfunctioning, one cannot but have the appropriate perception. Various forms of restriction on movement, or bodily paralysis, are possible, but what we have established so far is that part of what it is to have the concept of objective states of affairs is to acknowledge this double causal dependence of perception on the states themselves and on the perceiver's spatial relation to them.

This very general a priori principle has to be applied in experience. It must be possible, for each kind of feature f, to learn by experience what sort of relation to the state of f's obtaining is needed for one to perceive it. And it must also be possible to manifest possession of such knowledge. In ordinary child-development the manifestation consists in doing something at least as much as in saying anything, and the learning comes from simultaneously exploring the possibilities of, and results of, one's voluntary bodily movements. We note one degree of development when the infant can put his hand under the blanket to retrieve a toy which he has just seen disappear under there; we attribute another when the child can, in response to the question 'Is the cat in the kitchen?', go there, look around in every likely hiding-place, and come back with the appropriate report. The learning and use of language in general, and of spatial and perceptual language in particular, is typically by language-games.[88]

But how far are these familiar and pervasive facts necessary? Could it ever make sense to attribute spatial and perceptual concepts to a creature which had no control at all over what it perceives? We can imagine someone totally paralysed except for speech (even down to eyelids and eyeballs), and lacking any willing helpers to respond to his requests for a change of scene, yet able to say where he is, and even to explain how his perceptions depend on his position. But the ease of conceiving this surely depends on our supposing the patient to have acquired and demonstrated mastery of the relevant concepts in the normal active way, and to retain, in some second-order sense, the dispositions for the appropriate bodily actions, if only his paralysis could be relieved.

What we have to ask ourselves is whether we can attribute perception of objective states, and knowledge of spatial relations, to a being which never had any control over its position and perceptual intake. Such a creature would be unable to make any distinction between changes in its experience which were (at least partly) due to its initiation, and changes which simply occur. It could never do a "double-take", for it could not <u>take</u> a second look at something; it could never deliberately survey a house from top to bottom, and then again from bottom to top. Thus it could not use the criterion of voluntary reversibility of perceptions to distinguish the successive perception of unchanging, coexisting states from the (equally successive) perception of a series of objectively changing states.[89] If it thus had no control over the instantiations of the second clause in the general schema: If $\underline{f}$ obtains at $\underline{s}$ at $\underline{t}$, and one is suitably related to $\underline{s}$ at $\underline{t}$, then one has perceptual experience of $\underline{f}$ at $\underline{t}$; how could this passive creature ever learn particular empirical laws of this form?[90]

How could a being incapable of action <u>manifest</u> its understanding of perceptual and spatial relations? Could we reasonably attribute perceptions to a tree, or to a moon-exploring machine which sends back "reports" of what it "sees"? The trouble with plants is not just that they don't move around, but that they don't even <u>do</u> anything in the spots in which they are rooted; their leaves may shake in the wind, but they don't <u>shake</u> their leaves. Admittedly, a flower may open when and only when the sun is shining, and this may serve some need it has, such as pollination, but we do not describe it as perceiving that the sun is shining, nor as desiring to achieve pollination. In the case of the robot plonked on the moon, even if it could send back messages in English about its environment, rather than just television pictures, we can hardly ascribe perceptions to it, since it presumably has no desires which would explain why it bothers to make any particular perceptual "reports". It would be like an exaggeration of one of those personality-types one sometimes meets - either she who unrestrainably blurts out <u>everything</u>

she sees (and has the vocabulary to formulate), or he who will come out with an assertion only in response to a specific question. There is an absence of selectivity or spontaneity both in an incessant flow of speech, and in its production only in response to stimuli. Even speech-acts have to be <u>acts</u>, done for some purpose, to further some goal of the speaker.

Perception, desire, and action must (by definition) interact in the following holistic way - that any one perception can, in combination with a range of desires (which may come and go over time), explain a variety of actions; and any one desire can, in combination with various perceptions, explain a number of different actions. The relevant <u>a priori</u> principle is that, under certain conditions covering the agent's abilities, <u>if he desires that p, and perceives that the situation is such that if he ϕ 's then p will come about, then he ϕ 's.</u>[91] If the notion of perception enjoys categorial status, then so too must the notions of desire and action.

So our <u>a priori</u> concepts of other people involve our ability to interpret their actions, explaining them in terms of beliefs and desires, and in particular to interpret their speech-acts, for which we must add attributions of meaning as well as of belief and desire (cf. 3.12). Naturally, this does not mean that we cannot be puzzled about what to say of a given action, or even of most of the actions of an eccentric human being, a foreign culture or an alien species. But unless we at least hold our scheme of action-explanation in readiness to apply to a given individual, allowing that it must somehow apply even if we do not yet see how, we are not treating that individual as a rational being, capable of perception and judgment. Whether this stance towards another creature is compatible with treating all his bodily states as subject to causal explanation is a question we must confront later.

6.2 SELF-KNOWLEDGE

There is something peculiarly confusing about our awareness of our own mental states. Some philosophers have taken such awareness as the paradigm of certainty, and the only firm foundation on which all other knowledge can rest.[92] Others, reacting against the sceptical problems which have sprung from this approach, have been led to deny that there is anything that should be called 'knowledge' here at all, and to suggest that utterances apparently about the utterer's mental states cannot even be statements having truth-values.[93] By implication, we have already rejected both approaches, for we have asserted the reciprocal dependence of self-ascription and other-ascription of mental states. But it remains for us to give some account of the peculiar features of (present-tense) self-ascription, its apparent incorrigibility and self-evidence. Can there be justified assertion or judgment about undoubtedly contingent, changeable states of affairs, which is nevertheless not subject to the errors and ignorance which bedevil ordinary perception and judgment?

6.21 The Embodied Person

The apparent truth that, for a whole range of states (traditionally designated by the term 'mental') I judge that I am ϕ if and only if I am indeed ϕ is all too easily misinterpreted. The fact that the 'I think' is capable of accompanying any of my representations has led to metaphysical illusion. Four grammatical features of the term

'I' - that it is the subject of sentences expressing self-ascriptions; that it has no internal structure (nor seems to be synonymous with any complex phrase); that it is the subject of a series of different self-ascriptions; and that it is not even synonymous with 'my body' - might be taken to imply that each person has some sort of immediate knowledge of his own "soul" as (respectively) something which is a substance, which is simple or indivisible, which persists through time, and which can exist apart from the body.

But the inference in each case is fallacious, a "paralogism".[94] Such statements, if they are to have any determinate content, require the applicability of some criterion of identity, to distinguish the supposed object from all others and re-identify it as the same thing on different occasions. If there are truths about the identity and properties of the soul, they must, like all facts, be open (in principle) to ratification by anyone. The relevant criterion of identity must be <u>applicable</u>, and how else but on the basis of some kind of perception?[95]

The grammatical facts about 'I' can, however, with suitable supplementation, point us in the direction of concepts and criteria we do apply (and, it can be argued, <u>must</u> apply). The necessary truth (argued for in 4.4 and 6.11) that what I can assert by saying 'I am ϕ ' can also be asserted by someone else by saying 'L.S. is ϕ ', or (when appropriately positioned) 'You are ϕ ', or 'That person over there is ϕ ', shows that the reference of 'I' is not an immaterial soul, but a person with a perceptible material body occupying a position in space.[96] We can therefore conclude that it is necessary that people, being perceivers and agents, have bodies; the notion of disembodied thought, perception, and agency is incoherent, even as a secondary or parasitical concept.[97]   All this does not settle the vexed question of the exact relation between the criteria of bodily identity and of personal identity, but it does show that even if they are not the same, the latter is just as much a public matter as the former: it must be a criterion which we can apply to each other.

6.22 **Inner Sense**

When I say 'I am ϕ ', then, I refer to the embodied person which others can perceive, and the predicate ' ϕ ' in this context means the same as it does on the lips of others, and when I apply it to them.   The sentence has the same unambiguous two-part structure for all speakers: how else could it be a sentence of the language at all? If I can use it to express a judgment, it must be possible, as we have seen, for others to determine whether I am following the standard rule (or any rule), whether, that is, I use the sentence with its standard meaning (or with any meaning). But for many cases of ' ϕ ', it seems that the way in which I know (or, if that is putting it too strongly, what entitles me to assert) that I am ϕ is essentially different from the ways in which others can know it. They have to perceive my behaviour and interpret my speech-acts, but I do not. If our approach is correct, this must be so, but a philosophical problem remains about how it can be so.

A long-standing response to this problem suggests that a subject's awareness of his own mental states is analogous to perception of things distinct from himself, being another species of the same genus.   The terms 'reflection', 'inner sense', and 'introspection' have been used for the former, and labels such as 'sensation', 'outer sense', or 'perception' for the latter.[98] But if any such suggestion is to be accepted, we must explain the points of similarity and dissimilarity in the analogy; that is, say what is common to the genus and different in the species.

What has been called bodily perception,[99] including kinaesthetic and proprioceptive sensations, provides an interesting intermediate case which can help us clarify the issues. Each of us can normally say, without stopping to look, explore, or think, what is the orientation of his limbs relative to his trunk, which parts of his body are moving relative to the rest, and which direction is down (relative to the prevailing gravitational field).[100] We can not only assert these things, but we usually get them right (their truth or falsity is, after all, very straightforwardly perceptible by others); what is more, we can do so even if the classical quintet of senses are rendered inoperative. For this reason the standard list of five perceptual modalities is often extended. But why should the extra items be added to the perceptual list rather than to a separate introspective category? They seem to be in some ways "inner", and in other ways "outer". The facts known by these means could hardly be counted as "mental" on any understanding of the concept; they are physical facts about one's body, which are as directly and publicly perceptible as any "outer" facts. Yet the <u>way</u> in which one knows them about one's own body is unique to oneself: one does not have to perceive them, as others do, by sight or touch. It seems that each person has an inner sense for certain outer facts about himself.

We might ask in what way this sort of inner sense is

unique to each person, indeed, whether this is necessarily so. Could I have this kind of knowledge of someone else's body, instead of, or as well as, my own? Presumably we require for this rather more than guesswork which might become so accurate that we begin to accord it the title of extra-sensory perception or clairvoyance, for in so far as this is conceivable it is equally so for any kind of contingent fact. We have to imagine inner-sensory perception of the states of someone else's body,[101] and for this we have to sketch some kind of causal connection between fact and belief. Given modern bio-engineering technology this is not too difficult to do: we can imagine radio links, for example, between the electrical impulses in relevant nerves.

We have clear reasons, then, for describing the cases considered as bodily <u>perception</u>, as (quite literally) inner <u>sense</u>. For the facts thus known are quite distinct from the sensing and judging of them - one can, in abnormal physiological conditions, be in ignorance of, or in illusion about, the position of one's leg. And the relevant facts are not only distinct from one's own mental states, they could even be states of another body; the uniqueness of access to them is only contingent.

6.23 Self-ascription of Mental States

Mental states as traditionally conceived (consider sensations, thoughts, and intentions as representatives of the three ancient constituencies of feeling, cognition, and will) can now be seen to be importantly different from the bodily states which are the objects of literally inner sense. One is not normally said to be in ignorance of, or in error about, one's own sensations, thoughts, and intentions.[102] Again, the uniqueness of one's access to one's own <u>mental</u> states seems to be necessary rather than contingent, for in so far as one tries to imagine artificial neural link-ups with another person they do not have the same result as in bodily perception. It is one thing to be aware by some such abnormal means (or even by telepathy) <u>that</u> someone else has a certain sensation, thought, or intention, but it is quite another actually to <u>feel</u> that sensation, or to <u>have</u> that thought or intention. In these latter cases, one has to say that the mental state thus felt or had is one's own: any pain one feels, any judgment one makes, any intention one forms must be one's <u>own</u> pain, judgment, or intention.

The model of inner sense as a special kind of perception, which fits bodily perception so well, does not fit our awareness of our own mental states quite so well. Yet our previous argument (in 4.4 and 6.11) shows that facts <u>about</u> my mental condition are facts <u>for</u> everyone, assessable by perception of my behaviour. This is the point of analogy with ordinary perception - there <u>is</u> a fact of the matter. But is there not a further analogy, for can't I be mistaken about, or ignorant of, <u>some</u> of my own mental states? Notoriously, other people may be better authorities than I myself about whether I am vain, resentful, manically elated, counter-suggestible, acting out of malice, angry, or in love. It is now high time to look again at our concept of "the mental". In 4.1 we took as a provisional definition of the <u>non</u>-mental that it is neither incorrigible nor self-evident (to anyone at any time), so our understanding of the mental since then has been that a mental state is <u>incorrigible and/or self-evident</u> (to him who has it at the time). But that definition was chosen as a base for our attempt at ad hominem refutation of solipsism in 4, and in the course of that transcendental deduction (and since - in 6.1) we have argued that mental states must also be ascribable in a third-person way, on the basis of perception of behaviour. Thus we have claimed the a priori applicability of various concepts of states of a creature - perceptions and desires, most obviously - which explain its behaviour. Surely this gives us a different conception of the mental? For there seems to be no a priori reason why anyone should have incorrigible or self-evident awareness of what explains his own behaviour.[103]

Now how we are to use the word 'mental' is of course a merely terminological question. But it is important to recognize these two potentially conflicting tendencies. The tension will erupt into conflict as soon as we have a case where we judge some state to be explanatory of A's behaviour yet unknown to him, and perhaps even hotly denied by him. Candidates are not hard to find - subliminal perception, repressed desires, unconscious intentions, even perhaps unfelt or illusory pains. It is not our business here to start any adjudication of such cases; it may indeed be that the ordinary use of the term 'mental' and the whole family of more specific everyday terms does not determine what we should say about them, so that there is room for psychological theory (if properly disciplined by conceptual analysis) to go beyond ordinary usage.[104]

What we must recognize is that the range of application of the notions of incorrigibility and self-evidence may be very much smaller than we first tend to assume. This need cause us no qualms about our argument in 4, for our conclusion there was that there must be propositions which satisfy neither condition; it does not matter if we now think that there are really very few propositions which are either incorrigible or self-evident. In fact, we can admit that, strictly, only propositions about what the subject now thinks to be the case, or is currently disposed to assert, meet these demanding conditions.[105] Anything which goes beyond this, and imports any kind of causal connection with outer states or behaviour cannot be incorrigible (or self-evident). Yet this may still seem to leave a mystery about how it is possible to make avowals (present-tense first-person psychological statements), for obviously one does not need to listen to oneself saying that one is ϕ in order to find out that one is ϕ .

But must there always be some kind of explanatory answer to the question how I know when to say something? Whenever we get down to perceptually basic cases, for example to the application of colour-terms, we have to accept that when I see that something is red, I have no answer to the question how I know that it is red, rather than green or any other colour. Why need there be any more explanation of how I know, when I am in a mental state, that I am in it?[106] The case is clearest, perhaps, for my own judgments. If I am asked whether p is true, it seems immaterial whether I reply with 'p' or 'I think that p' (provided the latter, pronounced with the emphasis on p, expresses full confidence, rather than hesitation, or contrast with others' judgment). No more is required for the justified assertion of the latter than the former.

The puzzle, if any remains, is how it is possible so to weaken claims to believe, think, see or remember that p, so that they are no longer vulnerable to evidence against p, but become, as it were, purely autobiographical claims about what one is disposed to say, what one seems to see or remember. They then have the same status as statements about one's sensations, and one's intentions. But, as noted, these are still statements of fact, about oneself, which are assessable for truth-value by others. Why should our ability to make them about ourselves, without any self-observation, require any further explanation? It is clear in the case of statements of intention, and about what one seems to see, that these are relatively sophisticated performances, presupposing concepts of successful action and veridical perception. But even talk of sensations can be learnt and understood only in the context of the typical causes of sensations and the typical behavioural manifestations of them. "Our inner experience is possible only on the assumption of outer experience."[107]

Chapter Seven

TRANSCENDENTAL IDEALISM

In 4 we argued for the necessity of there being a public, physical world distinct from the mental states of any subject of experience, yet our argument worked only by appealing to the essentially communal nature of the rules governing judgment. We shall now ask in what sense we have thus defended "empirical realism" only at the cost of "transcendental idealism".[108] In 5 and 6 we found certain principles of causal explanation to be implicit in any notion of perception of a public, material world; now we will inquire whether the persistent application of such principles does not lead us to overstep the bounds apparently set for our understanding by our analysis of judgment. Can judgment and rationality coexist with the constant search for causal explanation, or do they thereby saw off the branch on which they sit?

7.1 MEANING, COMMUNAL AGREEMENT, AND TRUTH

The most crucial step in our argument in 4 occurred in the section on following a rule in 4.32. We appealed to considerations about the meaningful use of linguistic symbols, considerations which we claimed must apply equally to unexpressed judgments, i.e. mental acts with specific propositional content. Any one assertion or judgment must be part of a practice which is rule-governed, in the sense that any particular act can be assessed as correct or incorrect. But the most basic kind of incorrectness involved here is not straightforward falsity, the failure of a judgment to correspond to the fact of the matter. For someone's assertion may be described as <u>false</u> only if we presuppose that he is using symbols with a certain <u>meaning</u>, making a judgment with content p rather than q. There must be a difference between using a symbol with <u>that</u> meaning and using it with another meaning (or with none), a difference between judging that p and judging that q (or not judging at all).

But meaning is use, [109] or, more precisely, any difference in meaning (or in content of judgment) must be manifestable in speech or behaviour. [110] So knowledge of the relevant meanings, and ability to make the corresponding judgments, can be shown only by someone's following the appropriate rule in what he says and does. And this kind of consistency or agreement must be primarily with other assertions or judgments rather than with "the facts" themselves. For unless there is a <u>practice</u> which sets a standard to which our linguistic or mental acts are to be responsible, there is no such thing as assertion or judgment. [111] Raw reality, as it were, cannot tell us what to say or think. (That the practice must be communally shared, or at least shareable, has been argued in 4.32.) Thus we do not deny the traditional (and practically tautologous) account of truth as correspondence, but we point out that it presupposes an account of meaning which relies ultimately on coherence.

The point can be illustrated by the case of colour-concepts, a good example for us because for most colour-terms no explicit rules or definitions can be given, and also because the colour-discriminations made by different cultures and languages are known to differ very considerably.

Obviously, we cannot decide whether someone's judgment about the colour of something is true or false until we know what colour-concept he is applying. Of course, with speakers of our own language we normally take it for granted that the word in their mouth means for them what it means for us, and proceed straight to appraising truth or falsity, explaining the latter in terms of bad light or perceptual defect. But we cannot be so confident with our children, for we are not entitled to assume that their production of the standard phonemes is manifesting the usual judgments until we have observed sufficient agreement of infant mouthings with adult practice. When we are confronted with members of a radically different culture the case is different, for they have, we take it, some system of colour-terms on whose application they agree (by and large) amongst each other, but it may be that some of their terms have no translation (either simple or complex) into ours, so that we can only learn their words in the way that their children do, namely by immersal in the relevant part of their practice, being trained simply by correction on cases. In any given language there is (ignoring the complications of vagueness and borderline cases) a fact of the matter about whether a certain colour-term applies in a given case, but it seems clear enough that there is no truth or falsity, no rightness or wrongness about a colour-concept, or system of them. A statement or judgment may "correspond to the facts", or be "justified by the nature of things"; a concept or language cannot.[112] Do we not have here a persuasive case for the combination of empirical realism with transcendental idealism?

But we should seek a deeper analysis and more precise

definition of our "transcendental idealism" before resting content with a slogan. We can start by recalling that in the standard formula for a correspondence account of truth, namely:

sentence $\underline{s}$ (in language $\underline{L}$) is true iff $\underline{p}$

the truth-condition $\underline{p}$ appearing on the right-hand side must be of course be stated in some language or other, called the "metalanguage", which may or may not be identical with the object-language $\underline{L}$. A similar point applies to the "axioms" from which according to one recent programme in the theory of meaning,[113] it is our task to infer such statements of truth-conditions. These axioms are of the forms:

singular term $\underline{t}$ (in language $\underline{L}$) refers to object $\underline{a}$
predicate $\underline{F}$ (in language $\underline{L}$) is true of $\underline{x}$ iff $\phi(\underline{x})$,

and we must not forget the ontology-specifying formula:

the bound individual variables (in language $\underline{L}$) range over the set $\underline{S}$. [114]

In each case what appears on the right-hand side must be a term of the metalanguage. It cannot itself be an object or property or set, a sheer undigested chunk of reality as it were. For even in the case of material objects which are small and manipulable enough to be set up on a page immediately following the words '$\underline{t}$ refers to ... ', the little tableaux thereby created could function as ostensive definitions only if taken in a certain way, e.g. as referring to the pebble, rather than to its colour, or its shape, or the set of molecules of which it is composed (presumably the latter set existed in scattered array before the geological creation of the pebble, and will survive its crunching into gravel).   Of course someone can take a definition in a certain way without being explicitly told to do so, and indeed it is an important part of our argument that all judgment and language-use must depend in the end on such unguided rule-following; nevertheless that it is to be taken in one way rather than another cannot be given by "reality", "the world", "the raw data", "the naked facts", "things as they are in themselves".[115] We cannot apply the notion of "language-independent fact", "unconceptualized reality", or "thing as it is in itself", for in applying it to anything in particular we would thereby be using language, applying a concept; at best we can only use it in making the general negative point above.   "The concept of a noumenon is thus a merely limiting concept, the function of which is to curb the pretensions of sensibility; and it is therefore only of negative employment." [116]

Can we do more still to clarify this combination of truth being independent of what any one person judges, yet not independent of what the language-using community take it to be? As the saying goes, one can fool some of the people all of the time, and all the people some of the time, but not all the people all of the time.   This suggests a difference in the ordering or scope of quantifiers, which it should be possible to make explicit. Our definition of (empirical) realism in 4.12 was $(Ep)(a)(t)Ipat$, where 'Ipat' means that p is neither incorrigible nor evident to a at t.   In more detail, if we use 'Jpat' to mean that person a judges at time t that p, and 'Cpat' to mean that $\underline{a}$ considers at $\underline{t}$ whether $\underline{p}$, and if '$\rightarrow$' and '$\nrightarrow$' represent entailment and its absence, while '$\supset$' represents material (truth-functional) implication, we can say that empirical realism about a certain class of propositions amounts to the assertions that for all $\underline{p}$'s in the class:

both (1) $(\underline{a})(\underline{t})(\underline{Jpat} \nrightarrow \underline{p})$
and (2) $(\underline{a})(\underline{t})(\underline{p} \nrightarrow (\underline{Cpat} \supset \underline{Jpat}))$.

Now the saying has it that one can't fool all the people all of the time; and recent discussion of radical translation has espoused a necessary "principle of charity" according to which most of what a community says (at least about particular observable facts) must be true.[117] This may suggest that $(\underline{a})(\underline{t})\underline{Jpat} \rightarrow \underline{p}$, which of course would be perfectly consistent with (1) because of the smaller scope of the quantifiers. (Can it be that the distinction between the empirical and the transcendental hangs on such a thin, yet strong, logical thread?) However, this last formula is really not very informative, for there is obviously no proposition which everybody is at all times judging (even the most unimaginative occasionally turn their attention from one topic to another). What might better capture the suggestion here is $(\underline{a})(\underline{t})(\underline{Cpat} \supset \underline{Jpat}) \rightarrow \underline{p}$, which says that if everyone who ever considers the matter judges $\underline{p}$ to be true, then it follows that $\underline{p}$ is indeed true.

Can we exploit some similar scope-shift to try to convert (2) from the empirical to the transcendental? Hardly, for we cannot consistently with (2) say that $\underline{p} \rightarrow (\underline{a})(\underline{t})(\underline{Cpat} \supset \underline{Jpat})$. But clearly we do not want to say this anyway, for it would rule out not only the possibility of mistaken judgment about p, but even of someone's reasoned suspense of judgment at a time when he feels he has insufficient evidence. It may however seem more attractive to assert:

$$(3)\ p \rightarrow (a)(t)((Cpat\ \&\ Vpat) \supset Jpat),$$

where 'Vpat' means that a at t can verify whether p. This is an attempt at formalizing the rejection of "verification-transcendent truth" which has been advocated as the implication of the insight that meaning must be manifestable in use.[118] And, now that verifiability has entered the picture, it may seem more plausible to assert the converse of (3), namely:

$$(4)\ (a)(t)((Cpat\ \&\ Vpat) \supset Jpat) \rightarrow p,$$

than the previously-mooted formula without the 'Vpat'; for otherwise we would be committed to saying (for example) that if all those who ever happen to consider the question of whether Napoleon was sitting or standing when he knocked back his last glass of brandy before Waterloo judge that he must have been sitting, then, it follows that he was indeed sitting, even if the only people who (perhaps much later) turn their attention to this unimportant question decide the answer on quite inadequate evidence.

We may thus be tempted to conjoin (3) and (4) and proudly assert:

$$(5)\ p \leftrightarrow (a)(t)((Cpat\ \&\ Vpat) \supset Jpat)$$

as our shiny new modern logical model of transcendental idealism with respect to a proposition p, or class of them. The truth-value of p would thus be identified with whatever it is judged to be by all those who consider it when they are in a position to verify it.[119] This would be rash, however, for a little further play with Napoleon's brandy will demonstrate the unacceptability of both (3) and (4) for particular observable states of affairs (entailment sets a terribly high standard to meet). Suppose there was just one person who was both observing Napoleon at the time and for some reason taking note of his bodily antics; suppose too that this observer did not know that the hero was unusually short, and on seeing him behind a table took him to be sitting when actually he was on his feet. Such an observer was able to verify the matter (a quick glance under the table should have done) but came to a false conclusion. Nothing depends on the historical distance of the example; the point is of course that for any temporarily observable state of affairs the truth-value of the relevant proposition cannot be logically equivalent to how it is judged to be by whatever set of observers happen to consider it when they are in a position to verify it. Just as any one individual can be in error or ignorance (about a proposition for which empirical realism holds), so can any finite group, however singled out.[120] Our symbols have not succeeded in giving us an acceptable version of transcendental idealism.[121] All they have caught is an unattractive ersatz which reduces truth to what a well-placed elite judge it to be; the group to which this cognitive authority is given are distinguished only by their happening to be in the right place at the right time, but the granting of such authority to them is objectionable all the same.

The point is even more obvious, of course, for propositions which are not about particular observable states of affairs, but are in some way more general or more theoretical. We accept that whole communities can be in error or ignorance for centuries, even about matters for which they have the vocabulary explicitly to consider, for example, whether the earth is flat, whether living beings can be spontaneously generated, whether the stars are like the sun only very far away, whether humans and apes have common ancestors. The community's judgment, in so far as it is given at some specific time by some finite number of individuals, however large, can quite clearly be wrong.[122] And of course we also acknowledge that there can be truths which a given community lacks even the concepts to formulate – any example of scientific progress involving the introduction of new concepts shows this. Our empirical realism about particular observable matters cannot reasonably be prevented from extending into a more general scientific realism about the nature of the world.

The problem, if one still remains, is how to combine this with the undeniable insight that the meanings of sentences, or content of judgments, depend on the rules which are being followed, and that the rules can in the end be given not by facts but only by communally-shareable practice. We have to be both empirical realists and (in this somewhat hijacked sense) transcendental idealists. "All knowledge demands a concept. But a concept is always something which serves as a rule. But it can be a rule for intuitions only in so far as it represents in any given appearances the synthetic unity in our consciousness of them. It is only when we have thus produced synthetic unity in the manifold of intuition that we are in a position to say that we know the object."[123] Our concepts are given not by reality but by what <u>we do</u>.

7.2 THINGS AS THEY ARE IN THEMSELVES?

The argument has been that the meanings of sentences, or the contents of judgments, can be given only by how people use the relevant words. Any attempt to <u>specify</u> the meanings of the terms involved, to give explicit rules for their use, will have to use other terms which (for the moment at least) remain undefined. But for any term, or system of them, for which we presently lack any explanation, we cannot rule out the possibility of someone coming up with some such definition or explanation. To take the example of colour-concepts used above, it seems plausible to suggest that using the vocabulary of physics (about wavelengths of light), of physiology (about rods and cones in the retina) and of the sociolinguistics of language-learning we might give an account of the various different colour-discriminations made in different cultures. In such an account the colour-terms of the various languages would be mentioned, but not used: the account would be couched in a metalanguage containing the suggested vocabulary, but no ordinary colour-terms. Thus underlying the playing of a community's language-game, there may be certain "very general facts of nature".[124] After all, perception (it was argued in 5.21) must be a causal relation; as must action (cf. 6.12). If we make judgments and assertions about an external world perceptible to us all, does it not follow that there must be some explanation of how this is possible? -an explanation (whether known, unknown, or unknowable) which lies in the truths about how things are "in themselves" and how we are "in ourselves", and which would (if known) show both why things "appear" to us as they do and why we "appear" to ourselves as we do? [125]

Some such principle of the constant possibility of explanation would seem after all to be only the consistent, systematic, scientific application of principles about causal explicability which (we have argued) are necessarily involved in any concept of perception of an external world. But this apparently reasonable demand of reason leads us into temptation. For it suggests to our eager understanding that there simply must be determinate truths about how everything is "in itself", even if these truths are presently unknown to us and may ever remain so. Such "transcendental realism" offers us an "absolute conception of the world",[126] which the optimists will say might one day be achieved by a "completed science",[127] or which the cognitive pessimists will claim (with some delight in the humbling of our overweening intellect) must for ever lie beyond our knowledge, in the realm of faith. [128]

We have here a kind of antinomy. On the one hand, very plausible principles about meaning and the content of judgments lead us to the conclusion that anything that can be said or thought must (to have the content it has) be subject to the test of agreement or disagreement with users of the relevant language. But on the other hand, the very fact of agreement in the use of certain sounds by certain communities calls out for explanation in terms not used in the languages under study. For no contingent fact, even about our own perception, speech, and action, can be held immune to scientific study. Epistemology can always be "naturalized" into physiology, psychology, linguistics, and the other sciences of human nature.[129] Thus in the effort to describe what makes description possible, we are driven from language to metalanguage. And to avoid infinite regress we are tempted to assume that the metalanguage (or the meta-metalanguage, or some definite language anyway, reachable by a finite series of such moves) simply "mirrors nature", i.e. describes things as they really or ultimately are. We are thus led into a "transcendent employment" of concepts,[130] a positive use of the notion of "things as they are in themselves" for which we thought we had shown that only a negative use is legitimate.

Such a conflict of reason with itself cries out for diagnosis and resolution. Fortunately we can see the outlines of the solution implied in the transcendental idealism to which we have already found ourselves committed. There can be no such thing as comparing a language or conceptual scheme with raw reality (things as they are in themselves); there can only be the explanation of one language or concept-system in terms of another - that we have agreed. If we also acknowledge that for any vocabulary or concepts for which we presently lack any such explicit explanation there is always the possibility that such an explanation will be found (couched perhaps in terms we do not yet have), that does not imply that there must at some stage be a stop to this potential regress. The necessary truth that all semantics or scientific explanation of a language can only be done in some metalanguage, far from implying that eventually reality is waiting there to be directly encountered (even if this be ruled out for us mortals), rules out precisely that thought as incoherent. Yet this forbidden transcendental realism has a way of popping up in many of our scientific and philosophical ponderings; there is in fact a whole family of antinomies which can afflict our systematically inquiring minds. Let us see if we can apply the insights achieved so far to get to the root of them.

Chapter Eight

ANTINOMIES OF SCIENTIFIC EXPLANATION

Provoked by questions arising in 7, we now attempt a systematic exposition and resolution of a certain class of antinomies, or conflicts of reason with itself. The class under treatment here will not include everything that has been given the title 'antinomy', for we are concerned with problems that arise from the nature of <u>explanation</u>, rather than from the mere <u>existence</u> of various allegedly infinite series.

8.1 EXPLANATION: THE NOMOLOGICAL-DEDUCTIVE MODEL

We thus need to be very clear about what constitutes explanation. Firstly, we must realize that what primarily is explained is a true <u>proposition</u>, that which is true rather than the event or state of affairs "in the world" which, according to traditional notions of correspondence, makes it true. We do not explain <u>things</u>, rather we explain why things are as they are, why they come into being, change their properties, and pass away. Admittedly, we may talk of explaining events or happenings, or indeed states of affairs, but we explain them only as <u>described</u> in certain ways; and to explain something under one description is not to explain it under another. Secondly, what does the explaining is also conceptual, being a set of propositions at least one of which must be unrestrictedly general (i.e. <u>law-like</u>, not a mere summation of a finite number of cases). Thirdly, the relation between this <u>explanans</u> and the <u>explanandum</u> must be nothing less than logical entailment. We have thus stated the nomological-deductive model for explanation so beloved of modern philosophers of science.[131] To explain a given proposition, we seek a set of true premises, at least one of which must be a law, from which it can be deduced. Given a "conditioned" we seek a "condition" (involving at least one rule or "principle") from which it may be inferred. [132]

Now the point which starts a regress, and thus encourages the growth of antinomies, is that the demand for explanation can always be applied to the explanans in any proffered explanation. If it is reasonable to seek an explanation of any true proposition, then it is surely reasonable to seek explanations of the premises of any explanation, and we have an infinite regress on our hands. This can be avoided only by saying that there are some true propositions for which it is not reasonable to seek any further explanation: the regress would then come to a full stop, after a finite series of moves, in such propositions (which might be dignified with titles such as "self-explanatory", "necessary", "first causes", or "unconditioned"). Both alternatives (infinite regress or full stop) are in different ways intellectually unsatisfactory, yet the defenders of each can make it seem quite plausible by the negative tactic of harping on the weakness of the opposing alternative. For although explanatory full stops have their attractions for many, they need to be distinguished in some way from propositions for which explanation may be in the offing, and the ways of doing this are typically theological or transcendentally metaphysical and run into notorious intellectual difficulties. On the other hand, how can there be an infinite series of true propositions? - clearly only a finite number can ever be known, so what right have we to postulate an infinity of them?

This, then, is the general form of our antinomies. There will be two species, according to whether the demand for further explanation is systematically applied to the singular initial conditions figuring in each explanans, or to the general laws, at least one of which must appear in any explanans. Perhaps the term 'causal explanation' is most naturally applied to the former case of deducing why particular events happened or particular states of affairs obtain, but laws can certainly be deduced from other more general or fundamental laws. Such theoretical unification, although fairly infrequent in science, is regarded as deeply significant; and since for any scientific law it is conceivable that it might one day be deduced from other yet-to-be discovered laws, the possibility of regress applies to laws as well as to singular statements.

8.2 TWO ANTINOMIES

We now present in more detail certain intellectual conflicts that still puzzle us when we push our demands for explanation into that conceptually insecure border-country that lies between physics and metaphysics.

8.21 Has the World a Beginning, and Are There Uncaused Events?

Consider any particular, specified, event. It happens at some particular time. If we are asked to explain its occurrence, the pattern is to give a preceding event (or set of events and states) as its cause, and a general law which connects them. If, as we are inclined to think, the demand to explain any given event in terms of temporally preceding events is always legitimate, then it is tempting to infer that there must be an infinite series going back into the past; for if any event were literally the first to happen (or one of several simultaneous "firsts") it could not, by definition, have a <u>preceding</u> cause. The human mind seems to have a certain natural recoil from such an infinite regress, but is this mere prejudice? Certainly it begs the question to protest "But how could such a series ever get started?", for the defender of infinity here denies that there need be a <u>start</u>. Yet the ordinary man feels that there must be <u>an</u> answer to the question how any particular state of affairs has come about, and we can give his insistence philosophical cutting edge by emphasizing the indefinite article in his plea, thus implying that there must be a determinate fact of the matter, a truth (or set of them) which however complex could in principle be stated at large albeit finite length in some language or other. The demand is for <u>an</u> answer, not an infinite and therefore uncompletable series of them. Even if we may never know it, the thought is that there must be a <u>complete</u> explanation of why anything that has actually happened has done so.[133]

But now of course the defender of infinity will go on to the offensive and ask what such a complete explanation could look like, and how there could possibly be a cause which was literally first. For if anyone (whether physicist or layman) affirms that <u>everything</u> started from some first event, a "big bang", it still seems to make perfectly good sense to ask "What happened before the big bang?" and "Why did the bang go off when it did (some finite, specified time before the present)?" There need be no embarrassment about answering "Nothing!"

to the former question, for to do so is simply to re-affirm that the big bang was indeed the first event, but there is an unavoidable intellectual discomfort about having to say that something physical happened of which there can never be any physical explanation.[134] Of course this is a point at which naive believers will gleefully seize the chance to invoke the name of the Lord as Lighter of the touchpaper of the big bang some finite time ago. But even if we leave the intrinsic difficulties of theological hypotheses for separate assessment, it is hard to see why we should be debarred from asking why the Creation should have occurred just when it did. Postulating such a point of contact between the immanent and the transcendent implies a physical occurence without physical explanation. So far, then, we have an inconclusive stand-off between the proponents of full stop and infinite regress.

We should note that a kind of generalization of this antinomy arises elsewhere than at the limits of cosmology; for if a stop to the regress is countenanced with an uncaused first event, may we not postulate physically inexplicable events at any time? We do not lack candidates for the role. (Human actions, it has often been claimed, must be uncaused to be free - but we reserve that topic for 9). A cosmological theory (not now in favour, but recently put forward as a serious scientific hypothesis) postulated the regular creation, presumably unpredictable in detail, of hydrogen atoms in empty space. And present-day quantum mechanics presents us with an all-pervading indeterminism at the microphysical level. But this has, understandably enough, provoked metaphysical controversy amongst the physicists. Is it just that we do not know the "hidden variables" which cause such events as atomic decay, or could it be that there simply <u>are</u> no such causes to be known? Both sides presumably agree on the explanatory success of the present theories which deal in probabilities rather than certainties; what they disagree about is the awkward question of how these theories relate to "reality", and here they are subject to conflicting intellectual pressures. On the one hand, it seems a reasonable demand of scientific inquiry to seek a cause of any particular event, even the emission of an α-particle at a specific time; but on the other hand, what entitles us to assume that there must be a cause, even when our best-established theory postulates none? Such questions about physics cannot be answered <u>by</u> physics.

8.22 Does Matter have Smallest Constituents, and Are There Irreducible Laws of Nature?

Consider any middle-sized, tangible, material object, or lump of stuff or pool of liquid. It can - with varying degrees of difficulty - be cut, broken, shattered, squeezed, pulled, poured, splashed, or otherwise divided into two or more parts. The process can presumably be repeated - but how far can it go? Of course the bits will quite soon become too small for our unaided senses to observe and for our gross fingers to manipulate, and even our best microscopes must have some limitations on their resolving power. The question that has provoked philosophical interest is not what we can actually bring about in practice, but what there <u>is</u> in there, contained in any portion of matter. Do there exist smallest constituents which are indivisible in principle - "atoms" in the most literal, classical sense of the word - or is matter as infinitely divisible as the space which it occupies, since within any non-zero interval smaller intervals can mathematically be distinguished?[135]

In the purely mathematical sense (whether the ifinity is of the order of the rational or the real numbers does not affect the present point) there is clearly no lower limit. Our problem is not about making conceptual cuts in a perfectly uniform piece of matter, i.e. such that no piece of it, however small, will differ in any respect other than size and shape and spatial position from any other piece.

Our interest lies rather in the belief that matter has a determinate structure, that as we divide it (in theory, if not in practice) we come at certain stages to discontinuities, where the small parts have quite different properties from those of larger lumps, and moreover the nature of the small explains that of the gross. Thus within living things we distinguish highly organized structures of organs, cells, chromosomes, genes, etc., and within matter generally we believe in the existence of molecules, atoms, and sub-atomic particles. In each case the typical behaviour and nature of stuff of a given type is explained in terms of the properties and relations of its constituents. As we go down the levels, the theory becomes more and more general, until at the sub-atomic level we are told that absolutely all the matter in the universe is composed of such-and-such types of entity, subject throughout all space and time to laws which are thus-and-so. The explanation here is not the giving of a cause of any particular event, but rather the deduction of laws about one kind of thing or stuff from those governing its constituents.

The regress we are concerned with now is thus of explanation of laws, rather than of events. The moves in the regress are small in number, and only infrequently is a new step made - on those rare occasions when an extra level is added to physical theory, to explain the nature of the so far smallest elements in terms of yet more fundamental laws. But the antinomy that grows out of this regress presents finite and infinite alternatives as before. Are there some constituents which are absolutely fundamental, in the sense that there is no internal structure in them, so that no future stage of science will be justified in postulating laws about any such structure? Or is it the case that within any elements which we may ever be led to believe in there are yet further parts, and corresponding laws, to be found? As before, each party can attack the other. The finite side may be embarrassed to be forced into maintaining that there are physical laws for which no physical explanation could ever be found,[136] but the infinite alternative makes a mind-boggling commitment to the actual existence of an infinite series of "Chinese boxes" inside any portion of matter. The former party may be accused of putting obstacles in the way of the forward march of science,[137] the latter of harbouring a mystical view of reality as having an inexhaustible yet determinate character which no theory of ours can encompass. (Who is on the side of the angels here? - it is not so clear, when one thinks about it.) We have another antinomy, an apparently forced choice between different kinds of intellectual embarrassment.

There is a generalized form of this problem too. We have asked whether there are constituents of matter such that the laws governing them are absolutely fundamental in that there are no further laws from which they can be deduced. But the logical possibility of such irreducible laws would seem to arise at _any_ level, not just that of the smallest. We hear of "emergent" properties which cannot be correlated in any law-like way with properties of smaller entities, and of "emergent" laws which cannot be derived from those governing smaller things. (Such talk is apt to arise around the interfaces between sociology, psychology, biology, chemistry, and physics.) Now any particular candidate for the title of emergence or irreducibility can presumably be defeated by producing a suitable reduction. Yet if certain laws of sub-atomic physics are underivable from others, it must be possible that some laws at other levels of theory might be similarly irreducible, unaesthetic though such a prospect may be to those who aspire to a completely unified and rigidly hierarchical science, with sub-atomic physics occupying the deepest and explanatorily dominant level.

8.3 TRANSCENDENTAL IDEALISM AS THE KEY TO THE SOLUTION OF THE ANTINOMIES

For each antinomy, there is the possibility of a cautious attitude which avoids commitment to either finite or infinite alternative, and simply reports the latest results of scientific inquiry, saying which are the events so far unexplained, which the laws at present taken as fundamental - and adding the reminder that new results may come in.

For example, a cautious cosmologist may realize that to assert that literally nothing happened before the big bang is to go beyond physical knowledge. He might restrict himself to saying that although there may have been all sorts of previous events (perhaps even an infinite series of contractions and expansions), we could not have any knowledge of such prehistory, because our present physical understanding of the well-attested big bang is such that no information of any sort could survive the bang. He would leave it to metaphysicians to play with speculations about eternal recurrence, or the infinite variety of the past, or even the sense in which the cosmos might depend (non-temporally) on a non-interventionist God. In thus sticking resolutely to his professional last, our physicist would be saying, in effect, "The big bang is the first event we know of, and, according to present theories, the first we <u>can</u> know of." He avoids sticking his neck out to affirm either that there was a first event or an infinite series. If he is super-cautious, he will gloss even what he does affirm with the reminder that it is only the best we can do according to <u>present</u> theory, but bearing in mind the various conceptual changes by which physical theory has got where it now is, we cannot exclude the possibility of striking theoretical change still to come. If a big bang hypothesis is most preferred today, that need not preclude a future return to some new kind of steady state theory, according to which, at some sufficiently general level of description, the universe has never changed, and there was no first event.

In the case of our second antinomy, a nuclear physicist who is determined to affirm only what is supported by empirical evidence and to avoid any metaphysical exposure of his neck may simply report that the laws governing a certain kind of entity (quarks, perhaps) are the most fundamental we now know of. He may add that according to present theory, they are the most fundamental we can <u>hope</u> to know of, since any attempt to split down further would require such huge amounts of energy as to be not merely financially ruled out in these days of government stringency, but practically impossible because observers and instruments would get melted down by the process. Of course (he will admit) our theory may change, but this is the implication of our best-supported hypotheses at the moment. To the generalized form of each antinomy, a similarly cautious attitude is equally possible. One may admit certain events as unexplained (e.g. in quantum mechanics), or certain laws as underived, without implying that they are for ever inexplicable or irreducible. Yet one need not, it seems, thereby commit oneself to saying that <u>every</u> event <u>must</u> have a causal explanation, or <u>every</u> law a derivation from other laws.

But is this cautious attitude a mere avoidance of the philosophical problem in each antinomy? To say that we do not <u>know</u> which alternative is true, and even that there are physical reasons why we cannot hope to get to know, is not to deny that one or other of the alternatives must actually <u>be</u> true. Certainly, there are other instances of contradictory alternatives of the form $(\underline{x})(E\underline{y})R\underline{x}\underline{y}$ and $(E\underline{x})-(E\underline{y})R\underline{x}\underline{y}$ where it is perfectly reasonable to profess practically irremediable ignorance of which is true, but where it seems there is no reason not to bow to the logical law of excluded middle and admit that one or other statement must <u>be</u> true, even if we will never know which. For example, either every existing one-year-old robin has progeny, or there is one which has none; and either every primrose flowering this spring has at least five petals, or there is one which has less. (The complete surveys needed to establish the existence of relevant counter-examples are impossible in practice.)

Obviously, our antinomies about explanation are different in some important ways from these examples, even though they share the same logical form, being representable as the choice between $(e)(Ee')(e'$ caused $e)$ and $(Ee)-(Ee')(e'$ caused $e)$, where the variables range over events, and between $(l)(El')$ $(l'$ implies $l)$ and $(El)-(El')(l'$ implies $l)$, where the variables range over laws. We have noted the pressures which push us towards a choice, and the disadvantages which make us recoil from each alternative offered. A mere professal of ignorance does not really alleviate the intellectual discomfort of the situation. We have to attempt a diagnosis by deeper analysis of the antinomial alternatives.

The crucial point is that our antinomies are about explanation, and explanations, as pointed out in 8.1, are essentially conceptual in nature - they involve logical relations between propositions, rather than empirically observable relations between things. Even if we treat events as individuals, and causation as a relation between events,[138] the statement 'Event a caused event b' still contains an implicit quantifier ranging over laws, for it means that there is some law (even if unknown) connecting a with b; in more detail, it means that there are descriptions F and G such that F applies to a, and G to b, and such that it is a law that all F's are followed by a G. So in both antinomies we are implicitly or explicitly quantifying over laws, and laws of course have to relate concepts or descriptions, i.e. kinds of thing or event.

Thus there is something essentially metalinguistic about any statement to the effect that there is (or is not) an explanation, a cause, or law meeting some condition. Existence-claims about robins or primroses, however difficult to decide in practice, would seem (so far as the present argument goes, anyway) to "correspond to reality", to be rendered true or false by the facts, in a comparatively unproblematic way. But what of existence-claims about concepts, descriptions, laws, theories, languages, or conceptual schemes? It is not at all so clear what makes them true, or even gives them meaning. If the range of the generalization were only over <u>actual</u> past or present concepts, etc. in some human culture or other, then perhaps the case might be assimilated to that of the robins and primroses, given a very generous assessment of the methodology of linguistics, anthropology, and history. But clearly our antinomies derive their puzzling power not from factual generalization over human cognitive achievements so far, but rather from an attempt to survey all <u>possible</u> concepts, laws, etc.

And there lies the rub. How could anyone ever be justified in asserting anything about all possible concepts? We can say (or think) something only in some particular language (or conceptual scheme); how, from within one, can we even attach meaning to generalizations about all possible languages or conceptual schemes? But, it may be said, is not this whole inquiry into the conditions for conceptualized experience, and have we not thus been committing ourselves to assertions about any possible conceptual scheme? We have indeed been exploring the (logically) necessary conditions of experience, and we are not, we hope, about to discover at this late stage that we have been attempting something incoherent. The difference about the antinomial alternatives, the incoherence we are now diagnosing, is that they presume that there can be <u>facts</u> about reality - <u>contingent</u> facts, however pervasive - which make it the case either that there is an uncaused event or none, and either that there is an irreducible law or none. They assume, that is, that there are facts about <u>how things are</u>

in themselves, independently of any concepts or languages, which make true certain contingent assertions about all possible future scientific theories. But such "transcendental realism" is precisely what our analysis has ruled out as incoherent (see 4.32 and 7). Transcendental argument, about the necessary conditions for experience, is (we trust) respectable; transcendent metaphysics, making claims about reality which go beyond the limits of any possible experience, is not. [139]

The solution to these two antinomies, then, is not to profess ignorance of which alternative is true, but to reject both sides, not because they are literally false, but because they suffer from presupposing an incoherent transcendental realism.[140] The cautious working scientist who wishes to avoid commitment to either full stop or infinite regress shows a correct instinct, but it takes philosophical analysis to show that the reason for avoiding such commitment is more than ignorance.

8.4 THE REGULATIVE PRINCIPLE OF THE QUEST FOR EXPLANATION

What then of those intellectual pressures which pushed us into the antinomies in the first place? Are they totally deflated if we hold resolutely to our transcendental idealism? The pressure came from that apparently so reasonable demand of reason - that any contingent proposition, whether general and law-like, or about a singular event, be explained. All that we need do now is to distinguish two interpretations of this "demand"; one makes it a statement that for every event or law there is an explanation, the other an injunction to seek such an explanation for any given case. The statement we have just condemned as concealing an incoherence, but the injunction is left out in the clear, as a perfectly reasonable guiding principle of science. "It is a principle of reason which serves as a rule, postulating what we ought to do in the regress, but not anticipating what is present in the object as it is in itself, prior to all regress." [141]

We must realize that this regulative principle bids us seek not just new things of familiar kinds (more robins or primroses to add to our surveys), but new theories, laws, and concepts. In searching for some yet more fundamental level of theory from which to derive the presently basic laws of physics, we cannot know in advance what sort of thing we are looking for (except under the very general description just given). Of course, to be accepted, any candidate theory must pass certain tests, to do with explaining everything so far observed and described, which it is the business of the philosophy of science further to clarify. But for the invention of new concepts there is no recipe - it is up to us.

Chapter Nine

ANTINOMIES OF RATIONALITY AND CAUSALITY

We have some further internal conflicts of reason to diagnose. Like those already dealt with in 8, they are concerned with the possible extent of scientific explanation, but the special problems now to be confronted arise from the systematic application of science to rational beings such as we take ourselves to be.

9.1 TWO MORE ANTINOMIES

These problems can also be presented as antinomies, with incompatible alternatives towards both of which we seem to be impelled by irresistible intellectual pressures. But we will see that the solution to them takes a rather different form.

9.11 Do Mental Events have Physical Explanations?

Consider any mental event. By 'mental' we do <u>not</u> now mean that of which the subject can have incorrigible or self-evident knowledge (cf. 6.23), but rather anything for which <u>reasons</u> can be given.[142] For example, reasons may be offered for (and against) an action or decision, and reasons can be given for (or against) a judgment or belief. Two corresponding species of reason have traditionally been distinguished – the practical and the theoretical; but for the moment let us deal with the whole genus. That there is a genuine unity in the genus is suggested by the common conceptual structure we can discern. We say that someone decided what to do, or came to a conclusion, for certain reasons; moreover we say that he acted, or judged, because he had those reasons, and we thereby imply that if other reasons had been given him, he might well have acted or thought differently.

But out of these apparently harmless asseverations, notorious conflicts grow. In describing an event as rational in the sense of being influenceable by reasons, we are led in apparently opposite directions. On the one hand, rationality may seem to exclude physical causation, for a bodily movement induced by main force, electrodes, or drugs is not amenable to reason, and is not recognized as an action at all. Even for mental events which seem to deserve the name of actions or thoughts, if they are produced by hypnosis, brainwashing, or disorder of brain chemistry they may well not be amenable to any ordinary presentation of reasons. It may seem then that 'influenceable by reason' and 'has a physical cause' are incompatible predicates. And yet we have argued that certain mental events, namely perceptions and actions, must necessarily enter into causal relations – remember those two a priori principles to which we have committed ourselves, causally relating position of perceiver, state of affairs in that place, and perceptual judgment made (5.21); and linking desire, belief, and action (6.12). It is surely no news to be told that physical stimulation of the sense-organs is causally connected with perceptual belief, and that possession of intentions tends to result in relevant bodily movements. Our third antinomy is thus between every event, including the mental, having a physical explanation, and some events – the mental – having no such explanation.

9.12 Does Every Explanation Appeal to a Physical Law?

As with the previous pair of antinomies (8.2), the second one of this pair concentrates on laws rather than particular events. For any physical law, it seems reasonable (as noted in 8.22 and confirmed thereafter) to seek a derivation from more fundamental laws. But the latter (if found) will also be physical laws, which may be described as physically necessary, but certainly not as logically necessary. All causal explanation, on the standard nomological-deductive model presented in 8.1, appeals to some such contingent law. But when we explain an action or a judgment in terms of the reasons for it, the relation involved appears to be (sometimes at least) one of logical necessity. In the case of reasons for beliefs, the reasons can consist in other propositions which logically entail the one in question. The relation between reasons and action is (notoriously) a bit more slippery – for one thing, an action is not a proposition and cannot be entailed by anything; for another, allowance must always be made for reasons against as well as for an action; but if a desires that p, and believes that if he ϕ's then p will come about, and if a has no countervailing reasons, then it surely follows logically that it is rational for a to ϕ, although a may still not actually bother to ϕ. Even if we recognize relations weaker than entailment here (evidence or criteria for judgments, good but non-conclusive reasons for action) these relations still seem to involve conceptual rather than empirical connections, rationality rather than causality. Our last antinomy is thus between every explanation invoking a law which is itself open to further physical explanation, and some explanations – those involved in the giving of reasons for an action or judgment –

being immune to this.

9.2 THE RECONCILIATION OF RATIONALITY AND PHYSICAL CAUSALITY

Our "transcendental idealism" will also furnish the key to the solution of this second pair of antinomies, in that we must again focus our attention on the concepts or descriptions in terms of which we present these puzzles, and shun the impossible ideal of things as they are in themselves, apart from all concepts of ours. But there are important differences between the cases. The two antinomies in 8 involved only physical concepts, while the second pair presented here in 9 are specifically concerned with the relation between the physical and the rational. We solved the first pair by rejecting both of the alternatives; we shall deal with the latter by finding interpretations under which we can accept both sides.[143]

It is crucial for us properly to handle the notions of event, explanation, mental, and physical here. We must first recall the vital truth (already stated in 8.1 and put to good use in 8.3) that explanation is a relation between propositions, not between things or events. So we cannot accept as it stands the formulation at the end of 9.11, for it is not events per se that can have explanations, but only events as described in some way or other. The other essential point is that the terms 'mental' and 'physical' can be seen as applying primarily to concepts or descriptions: a mental predicate may be understood (consistently with what we have said in 9.11) as one which imports rationality (in the sense of 3.3) to that of which it is predicated, a physical predicate does not. On this understanding of the matter, it is not ruled out that mental and physical predicates might apply to one and the same thing or event - a subject may have both an "intelligible character" and an "empirical or sensible character". [144]

Now we have the materials for the solution of our third antinomy. Instead of saying, as at the end of 9.11, that every event, including the mental, has a physical explanation, let us say that every event (including those with a mental description) has some physical <u>description</u>, under which it can be explained in terms of other physical concepts and laws. More formally, using lower case variables to range over events, and upper case for predicates or descriptions:

$(\underline{e})(E\underline{G})$ ($\underline{G}$ is a physical predicate & $\underline{Ge}$ & $(E\underline{e}')(E\underline{F})(\underline{F}$ is a physical predicate & $\underline{Fe}'$ & it is a law that all $\underline{F}$'s are followed by a $\underline{G}$)).

And instead of saying that some events (the mental ones) have no physical explanation, we should say that some events have mental descriptions under which they have no explanation in terms of physical concepts and laws, i.e.:

$(E\underline{e})(E\underline{G})$ is a mental predicate & $\underline{Ge}$ & $-(E\underline{e}')(E\underline{F})(\underline{F}$ is a physical predicate & $\underline{Fe}'$ & it is a law that all $\underline{F}$'s are followed by a $\underline{G}$)).

This, of course, is only the logical form of a solution. We have given interpretations under which the alternatives in our third antinomy are not incompatible after all. But we have not given any positive reason why we should assert either of them.   Both formulas, indeed, might be accused of overstepping the limits set by our transcendental idealism, because of their quantifiers ranging over descriptions or concepts (all <u>possible</u> concepts?).   However, we can envisage interpretations which stay within the bounds of sense, for the second-order variables could be restricted to the physical and mental concepts within some specific conceptual scheme. For example, we can imagine some future stage of neuro-physiological science at which a vocabulary of physiological concepts is available such that every bodily event thus described has a causal explanation in that vocabulary. (It is plausible, indeed, to suppose that the parallel situation already holds for computer hardware and the vocabulary of physics and micro-electronics.) We can also see that in such a situation, it <u>need not</u> be the case that there are any laws which relate mental and physiological descriptions (or programming and electronic vocabulary) in the strict, exceptionless way meant by the use of the term 'law' in the formulas above. Moreover, there are conceptual reasons why there <u>cannot</u> be any such psycho-physical laws - one basic argument for this starts from the thought that any mental, i.e. rational, feature could presumably be instantiated or embodied in a variety of physically different systems, what matters being function and structure rather than material constitution.[145]   If this is right, the second formula above <u>must</u> be true (given that there <u>are</u> events with mental descriptions).

If there cannot be psycho-physical laws, then we can give reason to accept the first formula above also, with the event-variable '<u>e</u>' ranging over all events, including those with mental descriptions. That is, we can argue for a certain non-reductionist kind of materialism, according to which every mental event (i.e. one with at least one mental description) has a physical description, and therefore counts as a physical event. The conclusion deserves the title 'non-reductionist' because it is not merely consistent with, but is actually deducible from, the assumption (which of course needs independent support) that there cannot be psycho-physical laws relating mental and physical descriptions. The other two premisses required are that any mental event is causally related to some physical event, and that where there is a causal relation between two particular events, there must be a law relating descriptions which apply to those events. The argument goes as follows: consider any mental event; it is causally related to some physical event, so that relation must be covered by a law, but that law cannot be psycho-physical, so it must be couched purely in physical vocabulary, and so the mental event has a physical description.[146] "If reason has causality with respect to appearances, then reason though it be, it must none the less exhibit an empirical character; for every cause presupposes a rule according to which certain appearances follow as effect, and every rule requires uniformity in the effects."[147] Rationality is necessarily embodied.

This conclusion is deduced from the causal connection between the rational and the physical, together with the special logical character of our concepts of the rational. Our fourth antinomy, presented in 9.12, arises from that special character. The problem concerns the laws involved in explanations: must they always be contingent and therefore open to further physical explanation, or may they sometimes be logically necessary? It is easy now to see how to accept both alternatives, by distinguishing different senses of 'explanation' and 'law'. Clearly, there is a difference between laws of nature, which are logically contingent even if physically necessary, and laws of logic which must of course be logically necessary. In the nomological-deductive model of explanation, the laws appealed to are contingent, and thus open to further explanation in terms of other contingent laws, hence the possibility of regress discussed in 8.22. But when we give reasons for an action or judgment, the relation involved is either logical entailment or some weaker relation of rational support, such that it is not a contingent matter whether reasons of the relevant kind support an action or judgment of the relevant sort, even if the support be defeasible in any one case. The "laws" involved in such reason-giving explanation are laws of logic (or of criteria or evidence, or practical reason) and so they are not themselves subject to explanation in the sense of being derived from further contingent laws.

We thus distinguish two quite distinct species of explanation, the nomological-deductive kind typical of the physical sciences, and the reason-giving kind typical of the everyday understanding and justification of human thought and action. The latter, it can be argued, must be ineliminably present in any study which deserves the name of social science.[148] When we explain someone's decisions or judgments in terms of his reasons, we are not only performing reasoning ourselves, we are attributing to the subject concerned sufficient rationality to realize that certain considerations constitute reasons for the relevant action or belief. We thus treat him as a "rational being".[149] Being rational is assuredly a necessary condition of being a person, a topic and author of moral judgments. Whether it is a sufficient condition is another story.

Chapter 1 **NECESSARY CONDITIONS FOR EXPERIENCE**

1   See A156-8/B195-7; cf. A93-4/B126, A217/B264. These numbers refer, as usual, to the pages of the 1st and 2nd editions of Kant's Critique of Pure Reason. Quotations will be from the translation by Norman Kemp Smith (London: Macmillan, 2nd impression, 1933).

2   Amended from L. Wittgenstein, Philosophical Investigations (Oxford: Blackwell, 1953), 90; cf. A12-13/B26.

3   See A15/B29, A19/B33, A50/B74.

4   Adapted from A51/B75.

5   See A94/B126, A11-12/B25; cf. R. C. S. Walker, Kant (London: Routledge, 1978), Ch. II.

6   Descartes, in his search for an indubitable starting-point, allows us this much: "What then am I? A conscious being. What is that? A being that doubts, understands, asserts, denies, is willing, is unwilling; further, that has sense and imagination." (Second Meditation.)

7   See B2-3.

8   As Descartes did, thus provoking three centuries of attempts to escape from this solipsistic starting-point.

9   I am not unaware of the considerable recent discussion of the nature of transcendental arguments, represented for example in Transcendental Arguments and Science, eds. P. Bieri et al. (Dordrecht: Reidel, 1979), and continued in an Anglo-German conference on the subject in Cambridge in September 1981. But I am here attempting to produce transcendental arguments rather than discuss their

possibility.

10   As Kant (misleadingly) says he is doing at B19.

11   In the Prolegomena, §§ 4-5, Kant claims to be following the analytic or regressive method, by which one finds necessary conditions (those "under which alone something is possible") for something already given as possible; he contrasts this with the synthetic or progressive method used in the first Critique, by which one gives sufficient conditions for something and thereby demonstrates that it is possible (indeed actual).   If it is synthetic a priori propositions that we are talking about, this distinction of method does apply to the two works.   In the Critique, despite what he says in Sections V and VI of the Introduction - which were adapted from the Prolegomena and added in B - he tries to show that certain principles (e.g. those of the Analogies) have synthetic a priori status.   What has confused commentators (and perhaps Kant himself) is that these latter arguments proceed by applying the analytic method to experience.

12   Cf. Hume's Treatise of Human Nature.

13   Cf. R. G. Collingwood, Metaphysics (Oxford: Clarendon Press, 1940), Ch. V.

14   Cf. Wittgenstein, On Certainty (Oxford: Blackwell, 1969), §§ 97 ff.

15   Cf. P. F. Strawson, Individuals (London: Methuen, 1959), Introduction.

Chapter 2 **THE TEMPORALITY OF EXPERIENCE**

16   A34/B50-1, B67, A99.

17   Strawson, The Bounds of Sense (London: Methuen, 1966), pp. 24-5.

18   J. Bennett, Kant's Analytic (Cambridge: Cambridge University Press, 1966), p. 49.

19   Walker, op. cit., III.3; R. Harrison, On What There Must Be (Oxford: Clarendon Press, 1974), Ch. IV.

20   Cf. Strawson, The Bounds of Sense, pp. 48-9.

21   Cf. Harrison, op. cit., p. 90; Walker, op. cit., p. 35.

22   Kant himself acknowledged, in the footnote at B160-1, the artificiality of his attempt to treat sensibility separately in the Transcendental Aesthetic.

23   Cf. P.T. Geach, Mental Acts (London: Routledge, 1957), §4.

24   Cf. Wittgenstein, Tractatus Logico-Philosophicus (London: Routledge, 1961), 2.21 ff., 4.5; Philosophical Investigations, §136.

25   Walker, op. cit., p. 39; Harrison, op. cit., p. 94.

26   Cf. Walker, op. cit., pp. 35 ff.

27   There is nothing so silly that some philosopher has not seriously asserted it. But unless one can produce counter-argument to what one feels to be a paradox, its proponent can always claim (with Hobbes) that it is merely an opinion not yet generally received.

28   Cf. B71-2; Harrison, op. cit., pp. 99 ff., 112.

29   Walker's idea of associating various sets of thoughts (in one subject of experience) with different parts of his spatially extended body (op. cit., p. 38) makes no sense to me. What is the criterion of such association? And what makes all these sets of thoughts those of one subject? "Only in so far ... as I can unite a manifold of given

representations in one consciousness, is it possible for me to represent to myself the identity of the consciousness in (i.e. throughout) these representations." (B133.)

30 "In the present case I have no criterion of correctness. One would like to say: Whatever is going to seem right to me is right. And that only means that here we can't talk about right." (Philosophical Investigations, § 258.)

31 "Since brass, nor stone, nor earth, nor boundless sea
   But sad mortality o'er-sways their power ...
   ... who (Time's) spoil of beauty can forbid?
   O, none unless this miracle have might,
   That in black ink my love may still shine bright."

   (Shakespeare, Sonnet LXV)

   Sonnet XVIII ends:
   "So long as men can breathe or eyes can see
   So long lives this and this gives life to thee."

   Obviously, black ink and men's breath and sight are just as perishable (rather more so, in fact) than brass, stone, earth, and sea; the point must be that at any future time it is possible for minds to think of what has been.

32 Consider Plato's timeless world of Forms, and how Aristotle's subtle problem about judgments about the future continues to perplex us.

33 "If we were not conscious that what we think is the same as what we thought a moment before, all reproduction in the series of representations would be useless." (A103.) Cf. B71-2 and A137-40/B176-9.

Chapter 3 THE LOGICAL FORMS OF JUDGMENTS

34 Cf. Bennett, Rationality (London: Routledge, 1964), § 4.

35 Ibid., § 5.

36 Cf. n. 24 above.

37 We thus admit, from Kant's table of forms of judgment at A70/B95, "Affirmative" and "Negative", and (if interpreted in a purely truth-functional sense) "Hypothetical" and "Disjunctive".

38 Cf. W. V. O. Quine's "first phase of reference", Word and Object (Cambridge, Mass.: MIT Press, 1960), § 22.

39 Cf. Strawson, Individuals, Ch. VII.

40 Cf. Bennett, op. cit., § 8.

41 Cf. Quine, op. cit., § 19.

42 Thus I do not see that Bennett's "Describer" (op. cit., § 11) can coherently be ascribed the use of words for sorts of material object ('clock', 'log,' etc.) but denied the understanding of any tense other than the present. For surely the understanding of such words implies the ability to cope with sentences such as 'This is the same clock as was here yesterday.'

43 Cf. Bennett, Kant's Analytic, p. 207; Wittgenstein, Philosophical Investigations, § 265.

44 Cf. Harrison, op. cit., §§ 14–18.

45 We thus add, as characteristic of the "fully-fledged" use of language the following members of Kant's table of forms of judgment – "Universal", "Particular" (i.e. Existential), and "Singular"; and we insist that tense must be included in this conceptual package. Time is emerging as more and more fundamental to our inquiry.

What is a man,
If his chief good and market of his time
Be but to sleep and feed? a beast, no more.

Sure, he that made us with such large discourse
Looking before and after, gave us not
That capability and god-like reason
To fust in us unused.

(Shakespeare, Hamlet, Act IV, scene iv)

Ponder too the dark saying which appears on the first and last pages of Heidegger's Being and Time (Oxford: Blackwell, 1962) - 'Time is the horizon of Being.'

46   Cf. Bennett, Rationality, §§ 9-10

Chapter 4 **EMPIRICAL REALISM**

47   Cf. Descartes' second Meditation: "... at least I seem to see, to hear, to be warmed. This cannot be unreal; and this is what is properly called my sensation; further, sensation, precisely so regarded, is nothing but an act of consciousness."

48   My definition of these notions was suggested by D.M. Armstrong, A Materialist Theory of the Mind (London: Routledge, 1968), Ch. 6. x, and by B. Williams, Descartes: The Project of Pure Enquiry (Harmondsworth: Penguin, 1978), Appendix 1; but note that the latter's use of the term 'proposition' is tied to grammatical person and tense in a way in which mine is not.

49   Berkeley's, in fact; in the third Dialogue, Philonous says: "When I deny sensible things an existence out of the mind, I do not mean my mind in particular, but all minds. Now it is plain they have an existence exterior to my mind, since I find them by experience to be independent of it. There is therefore some other mind wherein they exist ...".

50 A proposition which Wittgenstein says "appears to contain the last consequence of solipsism", Philosophical Remarks (Oxford: Blackwell, 1975), § 54.

51 "The true solipsist is rather one who simply has no use for the distinction between himself and what is not himself." Strawson, Individuals, p. 73.

52 B131.

53 A103.

54 Cf. J.F. Rosenberg, One World and Our Knowledge of It (Dordrecht: Reidel, 1980), pp. 75 ff. But see R. Howell, "Apperception and the 1787 Transcendental Deduction", Synthese 47 (1981), for some extremely complicated doubts about the necessity of the principle of apperception stated by Kant at B131 and quoted above.

55 B275.

56 Cf. Walker, op. cit., pp. 115 ff.

57 Cf. A. J. Ayer, "Can There Be a Private Language?", Proceedings of the Aristotelian Society, Supplement 28 (1954).

58 Cf. Harrison, op. cit., § 18.

59 Bennett's doubts on this point in Kant's Analytic (p. 209) had not been resolved 13 years later, in his "Analytic Transcendental Arguments", in Transcendental Arguments and Science, eds. P. Bieri et al. (Dordrecht: Reidel, 1979), see p. 55.

60 I take Kant's talk in the Transcendental Deduction of the "synthetic unity of apperception" to be his way of considering the necessary conditions for judgments to have specific content. Cf. the fascinating footnote at B133-4: "... If, for instance, I think red in general, I

thereby represent to myself a property which can be found in something, or can be combined with other representations; that is, only by means of a presupposed possible synthetic unity can I represent to myself the analytic unity. ... The synthetic unity of apperception is therefore that highest point, to which we must ascribe all employment of the understanding, even the whole of logic, and conformably therewith, transcendental philosophy. Indeed this faculty of apperception is the understanding itself." See my paper forthcoming in <u>Kant-Studien.</u>

The formulation just given in my text makes it explicit that the time at which a judgment is made need not be the time involved in the <u>content</u> of the judgement, the time at which the relevant feature is supposed to obtain. This suggests the possibility of a further stage of analysis of the notion of independence, beyond that treated in 4.1, using the four-place relation <u>Iftat'</u> to mean that the proposition that feature $\underline{f}$ obtains at time $\underline{t}$ is independent of $\underline{a}$'s judgment at time $\underline{t}'$. The "reality of the past", or at least the independence of any proposition about a time earlier than the time of its consideration, would be represented by:

$$(\underline{f})\ (\underline{a})\ (\underline{t})\ (\underline{t}')\ (\underline{t} < \underline{t}'\ \supset\ \underline{Iftat}').$$

And the realism for which we are arguing in this whole Chapter 4, i.e. the existence of states of affairs whose obtaining is independent of anyone's <u>present</u>-tense judgment, would be represented by:

(**Ef**) (a) (t) Iftat.

61 Cf. Wittgenstein's famous discussion of rule-following, in the Philosophical Investigations, §§ 138-55 and ff. See too Kant's talk of rules as involved in concept-application at A105-6 ("All knowledge demands a concept ... But a concept is always ... something universal which serves as a rule.") and in the Schematism at A140-2/B179-81.

62 Philosophical Investigations, § 199.

63 Ibid. § 202.

64 See ibid, §§ 243 ff. - the so-called "private language argument", which follows, and seems to be an application of, the rule-following considerations of §§ 138-242.

65 "It might be said: if you have given yourself a private definition of a word then you must inwardly undertake to use the word in such-and-such a way. And how do you undertake that? Is it to be assumed that you invent the technique of using the word; or that you found it ready-made?" (ibid, § 262). See the following paragraphs too.

66 For a delightful presentation of the argument see Rosenberg, op cit., n. 54, Ch. IV.

67 The Bloomsbury group, perhaps?

Chapter 5 **THE MATERIAL WORLD**

68 A93/B126; cf. too A108-10.

69 B219, with Kemp Smith's translation amended by substituting 'juxtaposed' for 'to be constructed' as translation of 'zusammengestellt'.

70 See A179-80/B222; but whether Kant intended precisely this question of determining a quantity b from two givens,

or rather from three givens ('What is to a as c is to d?') is one of those maddening obscurities of detail in the text of the Critique. Cf. Rosenberg, op. cit., p. 47.

71 Detailed by Christopher Peacocke in Holistic Explanation: Action, Space, Interpretation (Oxford: Clarendon Press, 1979), Ch. I.

72 A182/B225-6 (The First Analogy).

73 R. Swinburne ("Times", Analysis 25, 1964-5) suggests that one could have experiences which were evidence for, although not perceptions of, temporally unrelated events. But one can take one's experience as evidence for p only if p is coherent, not a logical impossibility. In the myth of warring tribes which Swinburne supposes might be separated temporally but not spatially by the wave of a magician's wand - so that they occupy the same place but not the same time-system - our reason for accepting that any such trick could be turned is supposed to consist in what the tribesmen say after being "reunited in time". But how can we believe what they say, or give it a certain interpretation, unless we can coherently conceive of ourselves perceiving what our informants claim to have seen?

It seems to be essentially for this reason that Swinburne changes his mind on this issue (see his Space and Time (London: Macmillan, 1968), Ch. X), and decides that no such myth could disprove the necessary unity of time. Walker however persists with the fancy (op. cit., IV. 4), but at the cost of playing fast and loose with personal identity, imagining people undergoing amoeba-like splits and fusing together again.

74 Adapted from A186/B229 by substituting 'worlds' for 'things, that is, new substances'. Kant's move from singular to plural in his talk of substance in the First Analogy is another of those mystifying inconsistencies which drive his commentators to distraction, or at least to extraordinary disagreements. Thus W.H. Walsh declares "I find Kant's central argument in the First Analogy impressive, indeed unanswerable", in his Kant's Criticism of Metaphysics (Edinburgh: The University Press, 1975), p. 134; yet Walker on the other hand, concludes "Whichever way one takes it the argument of the First Analogy is quite remarkably unpersuasive" (op. cit., p. 111). I think that if one takes 'substance' in something like Spinoza's sense, to mean the whole material world, then one can side with Walsh here (cf. Strawson's Bounds of Sense, p. 130).

75 B234 (The Second Analogy).

76 The appeal to regularities within experience is of course a feature of philosophical empiricism from Berkeley and Hume onwards. It reappears even in contemporary philosophers who might seem to be questioning this tradition: for example, the laws which Ross Harrison requires for the possibility of judgment (op. cit., 18), although supposed to connect states "of the world", are introduced at a stage of his argument where no distinction has been shown between what is experienced and what exists. Again, Peacocke (op. cit., IV.1), despite from the very beginning having made the point that the explanation of experience must appeal to notions of positions in space and of the objective features of such places, tries to

demonstrate the applicability of a particular spatial model to account for a possible course of experience (p. 183) by what he calls "an empirical theory of regularity" which seems to concern regularities within experience only.

77 The senses "give us no notion of continued existence, because they cannot operate beyond the extent, in which they really operate", Hume Treatise I.IV.ii. "Objective meaning cannot consist in the relation to another representation ... for in that case the question again arises, how this latter representation goes out beyond itself ..." (A197/B242).

78 My indebtedness at this stage of the argument to Strawson's Individuals, Chs. I and II, will be obvious.

79 This is a version of Peacocke's a priori principle governing the holistic explanation of perceptions (op. cit., p. 16).

80 As in Strawson, op. cit., Ch. II.

81 So any object of perception must have some intrinsic quality which occupies some definite portion of space; we thus find reason for Kant's "Axiom of Intuition", that all intuitions are extensive magnitudes (A162/B202). Cf. Rosenberg, op. cit., pp. 22. ff.

82 See Rosenberg, op. cit., Ch. 2 for a fuller argument for the "conceptual package" involved in realism, summarized there on pp. 33-4.

83 See A. Quinton, "Spaces and Times", Philosophy 37 (1962), and T. Wilkerson, Kant's Critique of Pure Reason (Oxford: Clarendon Press, 1976), 2.3.

84 Plato, Sophist 247.

85 A211 (Principle of the Third Analogy, as stated in A).

86   Adapted from A216/B263.

Chapter 6 **THE MENTAL**

87   Cf. Philosophical Investigations, § 580.

88   We notice a convergence here between Wittgenstein, Heidegger and Piaget (reluctant as any one of them may have been to acknowledge it).

89   The distinction, and the example of looking at the parts of a house, come of course from Kant's Second Analogy. But it is not clear whether he intended to make anything of the difference between the voluntary reversibility of perceptions and the mere possibility of their occurring in a different order. In the Third Analogy he talks of my being able to "direct my perception first to the moon and then to the earth, or conversely" (B257), but in the Second he says "my perceptions could begin with the apprehension of the roof and end with the basement, or could begin from below and end above" (A192/B237-8), which leaves it ambiguous whether I can change the order at will.

90   If the empiricists wrongly seek law-like regularities within experience, Kant seems to move too swiftly to causal laws connecting non-mental events, as so many commentators on the Second Analogy have thought.   I suspect that the right course is to emphasize the causal connections between events and perceptions, and perception and action. Cf. S. Hampshire, Thought and Action (London: Chatto & Windus, 1959), pp. 47 ff.; and Sartre, Being and Nothingness (London: Methuen, 1956): "The point of view of pure knowledge is contradictory; there is only the point of view of engaged knowledge.

This amounts to saying that knowlege and action are only two abstract aspects of an original, concrete relation" (p. 308); and "The world from the moment of the upsurge of my For-itself is revealed as the indication of acts to be performed ..." (p. 322). Sartre's version of "the primacy of practice" can be traced back to Heidegger, and Hampshire's to the later Wittgenstein.

91 I thus hint at a transcendental deduction of a version of Peacocke's other a priori principle of holistic explanation (op. cit., n. 71 p. 11). See Armstrong (op. cit., n. 48) for more on the interdependence of perception and action.

92 Following the seductive lead of Descartes, of course.

93 P. M. S. Hacker attributes this "non-cognitive thesis of avowals" to Wittgenstein in Insight and Illusion (Oxford: Clarendon Press, 1972), Ch. IX.

94 Cf. Kant's brief outline of his four paralogisms at B407-9.

95 This is essentially Kant's diagnosis of the fallacy; see B411-3, 421-2.

96 "In my own consciousness, therefore, identity of person is unfailingly met with. But if I view myself from the standpoint of another person (as object of his outer intuition), it is this outer observer who first represents me in time, for in the apperception time is represented, strictly speaking, only in me". (A362.) But see P. Guyer, "Placing Myself in Time: Kant's Third Paralogism", in Akten des 5. Intenationalen Kant-Kongresses, ed. G. Funke (Bonn: Bouvier Verlag Herbert Grundmann, 1981), Sekt. VII.

97 For more argument for this, see T. Penelhum, Survival and Disembodied Existence (London: Routedge, 1970).

98 Locke, Essay Concerning Human Understanding, 11. i. 3-4; Hume, Treatise I.I.ii; at A 22/B37 Kant says "By means of outer sense ... we represent to ourselves objects as outside us. ... Inner sense (is that) by means of which the mind intuits itself or its inner state ...".

99 Armstrong, op. cit., n. 48, pp. 95 ff., 306 ff.

100 As the late Gareth Evans emphasized in his last series of seminars, in Oxford, Summer 1980.

101 Cf. Wittgenstein, The Blue Book (Oxford: Blackwell, 1958), pp. 50 ff.

102 This is the Cartesian understanding of conscious experience, which philosophers have assumed without question for so long. See Descartes' Principles of Philosophy, Part I, § IX.

103 D. C. Dennett has recently re-emphasized the distinction between what we have incorrigible awareness of, and what explains our behaviour. See his Content and Consciousness (London: Routledge, 1969), pp. 118-19, and Brainstorms (Hassocks: Harvester Press, 1978), pp. 30 ff. and elsewhere (see index references to 'incorrigibility').

104 See Dennett's Brainstorms, Ch. XI.

105 Ibid., p. 36.

106 Cf. S. Shoemaker, Self-Knowledge and Self-Identity (Ithaca: Cornell University Press, 1963), Ch. VI.

107 B275.

Chapter 7 TRANSCENDENTAL IDEALISM

108 This contrast recurs throughout Kant's first Critique, not just when these particular terms are used, but whenever it is denied that we can have knowledge of things as they

are in themselves, while asserted that we do have public, objective, scientific knowledge of things as they appear. Whatever Kant himself may have meant by the phrase "transcendental idealism" at various stages of his work, I am using it to mean something that concerns concepts and judgments, more than perception. See my "Three Kinds of Transcendental Idealism" in loc. cit., n. 96, Sect. XII.

109 See Philosophical Investigations, § 43, and passim.

110 A principle on which M. Dummett's presently influential approach to the philosophy of language is based; see for example the preface to his Truth and Other Enigmas (London: Duckworth, 1978).

111 Cf. Philosophical Investigations, §§ 241-2. Part VI of the 3rd edition of Wittgenstein's Remarks on the Foundations of Mathematics (Oxford: Blackwell, 3rd edn., 1978) contains further remarks on the role of agreement in rule-following.

112 "We have a colour system as we have a number system. Do the systems reside in our nature or in the nature of things? How are we to put it? - Not in the nature of numbers or colours." Wittgenstein, Zettel (Oxford: Blackwell, 1967), § 357.

113 D. Davidson, "Truth and Meaning", Synthese 7 (1967), and a number of subsequent papers. For an introduction to the topic see M. Platts, Ways of Meaning (London: Routledge, 1979).

114 Cf. Quine, Ontological Relativity Other Essays (New York: Columbia University Press, 1969), pp. 50 ff., and my "On What Sorts of Things There Are", Mind 85 (1976).

115 See Wittgenstein's discussion of ostensive definition in the

Philosophical Investigations, §§ 26 ff.

116 A255/B311-12.

117 Davidson, "Radical Interpretation", Dialectica 27 (1973); D. Lewis: "Radical Interpretation", Sythese 23 (1974); see too M. Hollis, "Reason and Ritual", Philosophy 43 (1967).

118 Such a formalization is one way of interpreting Dummet's explanations of "verificationism" or "anti-realism" in the theory of meaning. For example, he says "the fundamental tenet of realism is that any sentence on which a fully specific sense has been conferred has a determinate truth-value independently of our actual capacity to decide what that truth-value is." (Frege: Philosophy of Language (London: Duckworth, 1973), p. 466.) Does this mean that the anti-realist is committed to the entailment expressed in (3) ? Because of the ambiguities in 'we', 'can', and 'decide' (or 'verify'), I find it hard to tell precisely what Dummett's position amounts to (see n. 120 below). His other formulations do not help - e.g. Truth and Other Enigmas, pp. 146 and 358, where the question is said to be whether a statement can have a truth-value "independently of our means of knowing it".

119 (5) would seem to encapsulate the rejection of "objectivity" mooted by Crispin Wright in Wittgenstein on the Foundations of Mathematics (London: Duckworth, 1980); the rejection, that is, of any "conceptual distinction between how things seem to us when assessed by the most refined criteria which we possess, and how they may actually be" (op. cit., p. 7, cf. p. 197). But it is hard to be sure about this, for there appear to be at least three different notions of objectivity lurking within the

voluminous pages of that weighty tome, as the footnote on p. 355 suggests. Firstly, there is that just quoted from p. 7, which Wright seems to agree with Dummett in repudiating. Secondly, there is what he calls "investigation-independence" and argues on pp. 19-20, 32-8, 196, 216-22 to be ruled out by a proper understanding of Wittgenstein's insights about rule-following. (In XI.7 he accuses Dummett of illicitly clinging on to the second while rejecting the first, thus trying to occupy an incoherent middle position between the realism of Frege and the radical anti-realism which Wright claims to find in Wittgenstein. See too Wright's "Dummett and Revisionism", The Philosophical Quarterly 31 (1981).) Then thirdly, there is something which nobody will wish to reject for ordinary empirical or mathematical statements, namely "the general currency of certain standards of correctness and error" (p. 6) - presumably this is what is commonly disputed for ethical and aesthetic pronouncements.

120 It is a good question to ask who, exactly, are "we" in the various formulations of realism or objectivity (and their opposites) in Dummett and Wright. Every present speaker of the language? Past and future ones, as well? Everyone who could learn the language (i.e. in effect, all rational beings)? Or, narrowing rather than widening the class, should the "we" for "verifying" or "deciding" a given proposition be restricted to those who are in the right place and time to do so (as my formulas (3) and (4) suggest)? Further obscurities lurk within both words in 'can verify' - should they, for example exclude those with

poor eyesight and who have mislaid their glasses?

121 For a different kind of attempt to give expression to transcendental idealism in terms of modern semantics, see C. J. Posy, "The Language of Appearances and Things in Themselves", Synthese 47 (1981).

122 Pace Wright, op. cit., p. 220. The word notion of "community" suffers from the ambiguities noted in n. 120.

123 A collage assembled from A106 and A105.

124 Philosophical Investigations, pp. 56, 230.

125 Hence the Kantian temptation to develop a doctrine of "double affection", as detailed, e.g. by T. D. Weldon, Kant's Critique of Pure Reason (Oxford: Clarendon Press, 2nd edn., 1958), p. 253.

126 Cf. B. Williams, op. cit., n. 48, see index reference to "absolute conception".

127 Cf. the Peircian themes pursued by Wilfrid Sellars in Science and Metaphysics (London: Routledge, 1968), Ch. V, and which I critically discuss in "Things in Themselves and Scientific Explanation", Indian Philosophical Quarterly 8 (1981).

128 Kant must be numbered amongst the pessimists here; and this prompts us to observe that he himself was a realist with respect to meaning, for he seems never to have doubted that there are truths about how things are in themselves which we can never know (at least as far as theoretical reason is concerned). Our meaning-theoretic "transcendental idealism" is not Kant's.

129 Cf. Quine's "Epistemology Naturalized", in op. cit., n. 114. The principle was interestingly denied by T. H. Green in a series of three articles in Mind 7 (1882).

Notes

130 For Kant's distinction between 'transcendental' (approved) and 'transcendent' (condemned) see A296/B352-3; unfortunately, he does not stick consistently to one usage.

Chapter 8 ANTINOMIES OF SCIENTIFIC EXPLANATION

131 See, e.g., Carl Hempel's Aspects of Scientific Explanation (New York: The Free Press, 1965).

132 Cf. A304-5/B361.

133 Cf. A307-8/B364; A445-6/B473-4 (the thesis of Kant's Third Antinomy).

134 Cf. A427/B456 (Antithesis of Kant's First Antinomy).

135 Cf. A435/B463 and A524-5/B552-3 (Antithesis of, and solution to, Kant's Second Antinomy).

136 Cf. the passages cited in n. 133.

137 Thus undoing the patient work of "Underlabourers" such as Locke, who "remove some of the rubbish that lies in the way of knowledge" (Essay, Epistle to the Reader).

138 As D. Davidson does in Essays on Actions and Events (Oxford: Clarendon Press, 1980), see Essays 6-10.

139 See n. 130.

140 Cf. A503-4/B531-2; A528/B556 ff.

141 A509/B537.

Chapter 9 ANTINOMIES OF RATIONALITY AND CAUSALITY

142 This criterion for the mental in terms of rationality will coincide, I think, with that of intentionality which has been favoured following Brentano.

143 Thus although our two pairs of antinomies can hardly be distinguished as "mathematical" and "dynamical" in Kant's sense, the form of our solutions to our two pairs follows

his (see A531/B559).

144 Cf. A538-9/B566-7, and see Davidson's "Mental Events" (Essay 11 in op. cit., n. 138), Part I.

145 Cf. Davidson, op. cit., J. Fodor, The Language of Thought (New York: Thomas Y. Crowell, 1975), Ch. I. Dennett, Brainstorms (op. cit., n. 103), Introduction. But whether psycho-physical laws are impossible is still very much a matter of present debate.

146 The argument is due to Davidson, op. cit., Part III.

147 Adapted from A548-9/B576-7 (the solution to Kant's Third Antinomy).

148 We thus bring out a logical difference between erklaren and verstehen, the Naturwissenschaften and the Geisteswissenschaften.

149 Or "intentional system" (Dennett, op. cit., Ch. I). Rational beings, those capable of appreciating necessary connections, do not themselves have to be "necessary" beings, of course. Our fourth antinomy departs from the corresponding one in Kant yet further than our first three.